Your FAMILY BUSINESS
Your FAMILY NET WORTH

Strategies For Succession Planning

Gary Pittsford, CFP®

Published by Advantage, Charleston, South Carolina.
Member of Advantage Media.

ADVANTAGE is a registered trademark, and the Advantage colophon is a trademark of Advantage Media Group, Inc.

Printed in the United States of America.

10 9 8 7 6 5 4 3 2

ISBN: 978-1-59932-593-4
LCCN: 2015944769

This publication is designed to provide accurate and authoritative information in regard to the subject matter covered. It is sold with the understanding that the publisher is not engaged in rendering legal, accounting, or other professional services. If legal advice or other expert assistance is required, the services of a competent professional person should be sought.

Your FAMILY BUSINESS

Your FAMILY NET WORTH

I would like to dedicate this book to my wife for her help through all of the good and bad years growing our company, and to my two sons for all of the birthdays, ball games, and school events I missed when they were growing up.

TABLE OF CONTENTS

I KNOW WHAT YOU ARE THINKING —

TO WHO AND HOW DO I SELL THIS BUSINESS?

Through the years, I have seen that almost all business owners contemplating the sale of their life's work have similar questions. After decades of building value, they want to know: How can they estimate what the business is worth? Can they afford to retire? How can they safeguard their net worth and protect their family? How can they minimize taxes on the sale?

In the pages ahead, we will examine all of these common issues and a lot more, including some questions that seldom get asked. Take a look at the table of contents, and start your trip through this book with the chapter that fits you best. Perhaps your main concern is how to transition your business to a son or daughter. Or will you be selling outside the family circle? Maybe you are wondering about all those legal documents you need or how you will go about managing the cash once you sell the business. You may be wondering whether you will even have enough money left for retirement—how do you find out? And how do you put together a team of advisors to help you?

In my experience, most business owners have a variety of such questions, so reading this book cover to cover will give you the best perspective. I will show you how to get started and the steps to take along the way.

FIVE BIG QUESTIONS
TO ANSWER:

1. *What is my business really worth?*

Most business owners don't have a clear answer to this fundamental question. They don't know how to do an official valuation, and until they get one, they are more or less guessing. True, they have grown the company from zero to maybe several million dollars in sales. They have nurtured it and done a great job of running it. This is their baby—but to someone else coming in as a buyer, the business is only worth what the owner can produce in the way of assets and income.

Sometimes the owner is disappointed after we do a valuation: "I really thought it was worth more." But the numbers speak loudly. The valuation is based on three to five years of tax returns and financial statements, and it depends on usable cash flow, assets, and profitability. By examining the figures, a valuation expert who knows the industry can accurately estimate the company's value.

If that value is high enough, the owner might be able to sell and retire comfortably. Otherwise, the owner might need to work a few more years and increase his or her personal net worth before retiring.

Getting a sound estimate of how much the business is worth is an important starting point. We examine methods of valuation in Chapter 7.

2. How do I minimize taxes when I sell?

Business owners want to know how much they will have left after taxes, whether it be capital gains tax, ordinary income tax, or depreciation recapture. There are many ways to structure a sale that will keep taxes at a minimum, and you need to know about them. This issue calls for the expertise of financial professionals who have helped many people transition their businesses—whether to their children, key employees, or an outside buyer in the industry.

Some owners reduce taxes by gifting stock or the entire company to their children who want to run it. In return, the owner might accept a deferred compensation agreement, a position on the board of directors, or a consulting contract. Gifting generally isn't an option with a buyer outside the family, but taxes are still a major consideration in negotiations as both parties seek to structure the sale to their advantage. We look closely at tax issues in many of the chapters in this book, since they are of utmost importance in virtually all aspects of succession planning.

3. How do I sell inside the family vs. outside the family?

There is much to consider when you're selling inside the family, especially if there's more than one child. Business owners often are concerned about matters of fairness to all of their offspring, even if only one of them wants to take over the company.

It is common for parents to gift assets to a child, particularly if he or she has been working in the business or even running it for several years. Again, the tax issues are a major consideration here, as well as the retirement assets that the parents will need.

The parents might gift a percentage of the stock—for example, 30 percent. If they need more retirement income, they can let the children buy the rest of the company. Some parents have accumulated a high enough net worth that they don't need a lot of extra income and so are able to gift more. The tax code has specific rules on gifting, which your advisors can explain.

Taxes also are a big consideration when selling outside the family, such as to a key manager or someone else in the industry. You will want to consider the tax brackets, both your own and the buyer's. As you consider how the sale will influence the taxes or deductions on each side, you will be looking for strategies that are a good combination for both of you.

Those strategies, again, could include enhancing the seller's future income through consulting fees and other options. If you can't sell it for a high enough price because the profitability and gross margin aren't sufficient, would the buyer be willing to pay you as a consultant for three or four years? It's another way of getting more income for the seller and for the buyer to pay less tax.

As you can see, those tax issues play a large role, whether you are selling inside or outside the family. In Chapters 5 and 6, we go into greater detail on those considerations.

4. What happens to my children's stock if they get divorced or die early?

I hear that question a lot as parents imagine worst-case scenarios. It's not pleasant to consider, but they need to know how to protect the company and the stockholders. In Chapter 8, we look at how to do that with legal documents such as buy-sell agreements, wills, and trusts. It's essential that those be reviewed every three or four years to make sure they are up to date.

The children who are the recipients of stock may need to have the appropriate wills and trusts. Those documents are important not only to govern what becomes of the stock but also to protect the interests of the recipients and their families. Everyone involved must think carefully in advance about what will happen in the event of a death or the disintegration of a marriage. For example, if you gift 30 percent of the stock to a daughter, you likely will want to ensure that the stock stays in the family if she divorces or dies suddenly. You probably don't want it to go to the son-in-law and eventually see it end up outside the family. Legal documents can prevent that from happening.

5. Can I afford to retire after I sell my business?

Some business owners were frugal and made a good profit over the last 30 or 40 years. They used that profit to buy stocks and bonds or other investments—perhaps an office or apartment building, a shopping center, or farmland. They built up their net worth and now can easily afford to retire.

Many others, however, reinvested all of their profit back into the company and made it bigger, buying more inventory, delivery trucks, or whatever the company needed. After 30 years, they have a company that's doing well, but they have no other personal investments.

In that case, the question of whether they can afford to retire is largely dependent on the company's value and how much they will get for it after taxes. If a business sells for a million dollars and the owner has $700,000 left after taxes, that will bring in $35,000 per year if invested at 5 percent. Can someone live on $35,000 a year? And with few outside investments, if that business failed tomorrow, the owner would be virtually broke. That is why it is important to develop assets outside the business to protect yourself in the long run. It's not enough to have $100,000 in a 401(k) plan. We talk more about developing those assets in Chapters 4 and 9.

THE UNASKED QUESTIONS

What should I do next?

Once business owners decide to sell, they need to ask what they should be doing next to prepare. I emphasize that they must waste no time in getting things cleaned up. In Chapter 2, we look at what that involves.

Start cleaning up your financials. In the two or three years before the sale, make sure that nothing appears on your statements that would give pause to a potential buyer. Make those final years of your ownership the most profitable of your career.

Start cleaning up your personnel. Get the right people in the right jobs, and get your payroll down to where it should be. If your payroll expense is 25 percent and it should be 20 percent, it's time to get that into shape.

Clean up the premises, literally. Make the building look great, inside and out. You're about to go out on a first date with a number of prospects, so you will want to show them your best—that is, if you want them to take a second look.

In addition, once you decide to sell, you need to get a team in place—attorneys, accountants, financial advisors, and others. That can make all the difference in the negotiations and how well you fare in the transaction—and in your retirement.

How much risk should I take?

If you're going to take a risk, I suggest that you do it inside the business where you can control that risk. Whatever business you're in, you know how to control risk. You've been doing it for years. Once you sell the business, it is probably time to be more conservative with your profits from the sale and the rest of your net worth.

Once the business has been sold most people are concerned about their annual income and where it's coming from, protecting net worth for the future, and dealing with inflation, changing interest rates, and the stock market going up and down.

It's important to diversify your assets and have a conservative allocation which produces some growth for the future, but also excellent interest and dividend income.

It is important to protect your net worth, and you need to manage your risk in future years. We have more ideas to review on dealing with asset protection and good diversification in Chapters 4 and 9.

INTRODUCTION

The couple, now in their mid-70s, ran a hardware store in a small midwestern town all their lives. They bought it from the husband's father, who had operated it all his life, too. The store had been in the family for nearly 90 years.

The community depended on it. There weren't a lot of big retail stores around, so folks went there to buy not only just the typical electrical and plumbing supplies but also housewares—everything from kitchen utensils to refrigerators. They could even purchase lumber for their home and farm projects there.

The hardware store was a mainstay of the community. The town could count on the owner to support school and park projects. The store had approximately ten employees who counted on their jobs to support their families.

The couple was concerned about who was going to buy their store. "Our children don't want it," the man told me. "They've gone to college and moved on to other careers. My employees can't handle the purchase, and I need to find a buyer."

He told me about the schools, the local medical clinic, and the chamber of commerce. "I have to keep this store going," he said, "because the town depends on it." That's the way it is with most small businesses. The hardware stores, groceries, carpet stores, heating and air conditioning contractors, and countless others are vital to every community, small or large.

I could hear it in this couple's voices and see it in their eyes: They were concerned about their employees and about the town where their roots ran so very deep. They knew they were an integral part of it and were concerned about their own future. If they sold the company, would they have enough money to live on? The store gave them a salary—as long as they owned it.

Whether in towns or in city neighborhoods, people far and wide rely on local shops and other businesses run by families, and those families depend on their businesses for their livelihood. As the owners get older and consider how to pass the baton, they cannot help thinking about their security and much more. They want to do the right thing.

Those families—the husbands and wives and even the children who sometimes work the counters or help out in the back shop—might well devote seven days a week to their enterprise. Even after hours, there are still shelves to stock, inventory to order, and books to keep. Such is life at a small, closely held business.

People understandably want to protect all they have worked to gain. This particular couple had some specific questions for me: "If we sell, how can we keep the taxes to a minimum?" and "How can we invest safely so we'll have enough to live on and still have something to leave to our children and grandchildren?"

Money matters. Business owners may sincerely care about their communities and what will become of their employees—they don't want to see those people lose their jobs—but they also care deeply about what will become of themselves and their loved ones. No matter what you call it—transition planning, succession planning, exit planning—a lot goes into it. It's not just dollars and cents.

Over the years I have learned that part of selling a company is dealing with valuations, taxes, and all those financial matters. But I understand that in the seller's mind, a big part is also: "Am I willing to let go? Am I able to back away to let someone else make the decisions?" Some cannot. They've been in control for a long time, and it's hard to give that up. They put it off as they get up and go to work day after day. Succession planning involves a lot more than finances—it involves emotions, too.

THE TRANSITIONING BOOMERS

In this book we look at a variety of aspects involved in transitioning a business, including the tax considerations and income plans that were among the major concerns of that small-town couple who ran the hardware store.

There is so much more that people want to know: How can they find out how much they might get from the sale of their company? Will that be enough for their security without hurting the business? How can they structure the business and the sale to best protect their net worth? How can they leave it to the children while treating them all fairly? What kind of wills and trusts do they need? How do they set up a buy-sell agreement?

This book is for closely held family businesses of all sizes. There are 34 million small businesses in the United States, each with 500 employees or fewer (any larger than that, and it's not considered a small business). Many are much smaller than that: 26 million have only one or two employees, and about 7 million have less than a hundred.

Those 34 million businesses, of which 90 percent are family-owned, are often called the "engine that drives the American economy". They hire five or six out of every ten employees who get jobs. Family businesses generate 59 percent of the US gross domestic product. The 70 million people who work for small businesses constitute 54 percent of the workforce.

A great many of these business owners are baby boomers, now 59 to 77 years old. With all those boomers getting ready to retire, succession planning is more important than ever. At least five or six million owners of closely held businesses are likely to transition their company to a new owner during the next five to ten years.

THE ENTREPRENEURIAL WAY OF LIFE

Being a business owner never looked so good. Think of all those people who climbed the ladder for decades at big corporations only to lose their jobs in an economic downturn. They saw pension plans shrink. No longer would they be getting a big check every month for life, along with free health insurance and other benefits.

Those with the tenacity to be a business owner are often far better off. Entrepreneurs can control their own fate—such as whether and when they retire, the amount of their "pension," their very sense of security. A mid-level executive at some big company can't really do that.

When you own your own company, you control what is happening around you, even as the economy and sales fluctuate. You have a better chance of maintaining long-term income in retirement. And when you are the owner, it's hard to get fired. The entrepreneurial way of life is one of independence and initiative, and it can serve a family well for generations.

We've worked with thousands of family businesses over the last 45 years at our firm, and we have found that approximately 20 to 25 percent have children who will take over the family business. Another 10 to 15 percent may be bought by key employees because there are no children or the children chose a different career. And about 50 percent are sold to someone else within the industry. For example, some business owners might have one or two similar stores and want to grow into several stores. They look for opportunities as other owners look to exit. Someone is retiring, and someone is getting started. It's the cycle of life.

Owning a business can certainly be a good deal. A lot of universities have a four-year degree in entrepreneurship. If the students want to follow that path, I believe they should seriously consider working for a small family business. Many of those businesses don't have children waiting to take over and they are looking for a buyer.

A college graduate who likes the idea of controlling his or her own destiny and future net worth would do well to find one of those companies and work for it for a while. Studying, learning, and demonstrating their ability to handle finances, advertising, customers, technology, and a range of skills that are important to the owner is vital. If all goes well, it is likely the owner will give that young person a shot at buying the company.

For children who want to take over their family's business, we recommend a college education related to the industry, whether it's advertising, finance, retailing, or construction. Then, work for someone else for four or five years, possibly General Electric, Home Depot, Ford, or another large corporation. Work diligently and get promoted two or three times. Find out what it is like out there in the world, get some fresh ideas, and bring them back home.

That outside experience is important. It builds the young person's confidence, and it shows the parents that their son or daughter is serious, doing well, and ready for the responsibility. They will see that he or she wants to carry on this way of life. Then they can begin the succession planning process, which takes several years.

GETTING THE GROUNDWORK IN PLACE

When they are ready to sell and retire, most business owners will be 65 to 80 years old. Often they have postponed the decision for years because they don't know the answer to some critical questions. For example, what would happen to the stock if a son or daughter got 20 percent and then died suddenly or got divorced—how would the owners control the stock? They wonder about taxes. They wonder how to be fair to all three kids if only one wants the business. To move forward, they need answers.

If they have children, they need to ask themselves if any of their children could actually run the business. A lot of business owners are lousy coaches. They are good doers, but ineffective teachers. I have dealt with a lot of their children who are in their 40s and have never seen a financial statement or tax return for the company. They understand how to stock the shelves. They can deal with customers, vendors, and suppliers, but if they are to run the company for another 25 or 30 years, they need to learn every aspect of it.

What about that issue of fairness in the estate planning? I'm working with a couple that has four children, and all of them work in the company, as do two of their spouses. That's eight family members, total—and the couple wants to be fair to everybody. There are ways to accomplish that, but it can get tricky.

The owners of a business will want to make sure they have a secure and structured retirement income. As long as they have the company, it gives them an income, bonuses, and benefits. Those are gone once they retire. How will they replace them? We talk about a lot of ways that they might still bring in money, such as through rental payments, consulting contracts, or deferred compensation. Often the owners have never heard of such things. They didn't know that there are at least ten ways to get paid, each with different tax considerations. We can choose the ones that work best for the owner—the best income and benefits with the lowest tax. We design that plan by getting to know the family's situation and needs.

There are many considerations in getting the groundwork in place and so many excuses to put it off. The owners are worried and just don't have all the answers. That's not their area of expertise—and why would it be? They made their way in life through a business in which they had a great deal of expertise, but no one is the master of everything.

It can be unnerving when you're ready to retire and sell your business. You have a million questions, and you need someone with answers who can take you to step one and beyond. You need a team of such advisors on your side, specialists who can focus on different aspects of your situation and get things rolling several years ahead of time.

It's like going to the doctor for yearly checkups. If something comes up, you see a specialist. That is your physical health, and you want the best team. Your business needs regular financial checkups too—accountants, attorneys, financial advisors—and someone who can coordinate it all for you. This is your financial health we are talking about, and you want the best team.

TIME TO PREPARE

To get the best price for a business with minimum taxes, you need time to prepare. A sports team has to practice and prepare vigorously to get all the players doing the right things in the right positions. Likewise, planning for the final big game for your company cannot be done in a week or two.

You need to get the advisors and coaches together to brainstorm the particulars of the game at hand. Some companies are single shops in a small town; others have branches in multiple cities. Some include the real estate. Sometimes the children are involved; other times, owners are looking to sell outside the family. The questions tend to be similar, but every family and business is different, and it takes time to work out the best plan of action.

Getting the best price takes three to five years of advance preparation. If you want to sell your company for beans, it's easy to find a buyer quickly. If you want to get a good price, you need to position yourself and make your company look as good as possible. You also need time to position yourself and the buyer with a transition plan that is reasonable for both of you and that allows the business to endure.

The term sheet for the sale, sometimes called the letter of intent, outlines what the seller is selling and what the buyer is buying, how much it will cost, and the details of the transaction. When the buyer is one of the seller's children, however, the considerations usually extend to what works best for all, including any other children who won't be part of the business. And of course, Mom and Dad's financial security must be top priority.

The big question, then, is "how?" You might know how to run a farm, build a house, or operate a shoe store, but the lingo involved in transitioning a business may seem like a foreign language. That's why you need a professional team to draft a blueprint—that's the best way to make it work.

What most certainly will not work is putting your head in the sand. Unaddressed issues tend to get increasingly complicated. That's the consequence of procrastination. If the children were ever interested in running the business, they may well give up by the time they are in their 40s, even if they would have been naturals. They take their entrepreneurial talents elsewhere—I've seen it happen. Instead, I encourage the parents to slowly let go so that the child, or the children, can take over the business. Otherwise, it will go to an outside buyer, potentially a sad loss for the family and the community.

Every seller is different. You have to take into consideration your retirement goals, your charitable interests, and the activities you hope to pursue. Do you have a new career in mind, or do you intend to sit in a rocking chair on the porch and peel apples? Those questions need to be answered now because they will have a lot to do with your current personal financial security and your successful business planning.

The sellers who have devoted so much time and effort to the business need to develop something else to do as they back away and let the buyers take over. Will they become more involved in their place of worship? Will they learn to fish or play golf? Perhaps they want to travel the world or wish to share their perspectives on the board of directors of the chamber of commerce or a local bank. A lot of business owners have been so busy putting in 70 hours a week that they haven't had time to entertain the prospect of doing something else. The business has been their world, and when they sell it they can feel blindsided. It was everything to them.

By attending to that aspect of planning, in the years before retirement, you will avoid the sense of shell shock that can come from a sudden jarring change. It's all part of the preparation for a smooth transition of business and of life. It's all part of giving yourself time to prepare.

A BLUEPRINT FOR ACTION

In succession planning, we're developing a blueprint. In a way, we develop a time line by backing into it. Let's say the owner is 65, and she wants to be out in five years. That defines the length of the time line to which we can assign tasks. We know that at the end of those five years the owner intends to be signing a sales contract, and so we start backing up. What do we have to do in year four? In years three and two? What needs to happen right now?

I recently worked with a family in Wisconsin that has a 14-year time line. The couple anticipated that their son would be taking over in 14 years. Another family in Minnesota started with a ten-year time line, and it's now down to six. As time flies by, the family sees it all coming together. The blueprint tells them what should happen each year.

We develop goals for each year. We might be transitioning stock or improving the gross margin. We need to make the tax return look good. Every year for decades, the business owner was probably trying to make his tax return look bad. When a business is doing its taxes, the owner looks for any break he or she can legally get. The idea is to reduce the taxable income. But that's not what you want to do when you are trying to impress a buyer. You need to make the return look good for the next two or three years.

Everything has to be clear, because the buyer will want to see financial information that shows a growing company. The return might show that the owner made $5,000, but the company really made $100,000 once write-offs are added back in for things such as high rent and high bonuses. It will take time to position the accounting to show where the company really stands.

Early in the time line, the business owners need to begin transitioning the leadership—and that process, too, is something we discuss in this book. The transfer of leadership and the transfer of ownership are quite different matters. Whether a son, a daughter, or a key manager will be taking over, it will take a few years to gradually position the new leadership. If the time line is five years, the owners may decide that in three years, their son or daughter will be president. Meanwhile, the stock could still be transferred over eight or ten years.

THE URGENCY
OF STARTING EARLY

For most closely held family businesses, this is their first or second biggest asset—either the business itself, or perhaps the real estate if they own a number of warehouses or other buildings. A lot is involved in selling those assets intelligently.

Many owners have put all their profits right back into the business for decades, expanding the building and inventory and buying equipment. After 30 years or so, they have paid off their home. They have an IRA with $100,000 in it, maybe even $200,000. And they have the business—but unless they can sell it for a high price, they cannot afford to retire.

Some family businesses have grown to be worth $5 or $10 million, but most are worth up to about $3 million. Let's say the business is worth $1 million. The owner's income could be as low as $60,000, but most will have a salary of $100,000 to $150,000.

After the business is sold and the taxes are paid, about $800,000 might be left to invest. We might talk about taking out 5 percent a year for retirement income. That's $40,000 a year, and the owner, accustomed to two or three times as much, cannot retire on that. Since the owner has always thrown the profits back into the business, he or she either needs to sell it for a high price or learn to live very frugally in retirement.

That's why I advise young entrepreneurs to make sure they pull out some money every year and diversify their investments long before they intend to retire. I tell them to buy something outside the company, whether municipal bonds or stock in companies like McDonald's, General Electric, or Exxon. They have to develop a net worth in other places.

About a third of the business owners we meet have put themselves in a position where they have little recourse but to sell for a high price. They don't have other significant assets. That scares a lot of them, who worry about what will become of their family. For some, the "solution" is further procrastination.

Indecision and bad decisions create ripple effects. I have seen cases where the owner's daughter is the senior cashier, a job worth perhaps $30,000 a year, and he's paying her $45,000 because she's divorced with two kids to support. A new owner is only going to pay the cashier what the job is worth, so if Dad sells the business, it will affect his daughter and his grandchildren. He knows that, and it scares him.

Well before the day you hope to sell and retire, you need to be talking to your business and financial advisors regularly so that they can analyze your situation and give you some answers. You or your spouse—or both—could live in retirement for longer than you operated the business. You need to know, early on, how you are doing. Will you have sufficient assets to retire? If the answer is no, then you may still have time to do something about it. If you don't wait until the last minute, you can ramp up your total net worth to serve you well for years to come.

CHAPTER ONE

WHERE DO YOU BEGIN?

I recently worked with two brothers who had a building that was a combination hardware store and grocery. The town they were located in depended on them for food and supplies. The older brother reached the point where he wanted to sell his interest and retire. They talked about it for a decade but didn't know how they would do it.

The younger brother had a son who wanted to come into the company in three years. So we developed a plan to let the younger brother buy out the older brother and keep running the business until selling it to his son. That way, the business could stay in the family another generation.

Each year I deliver a few dozen speeches, talking to several thousand people. After each speech, people walk up to chat with me. There always seems to be a husband and wife standing there with something pressing on their minds. "We don't know where to start," one of them will say. They have listened for an hour and still feel overwhelmed. "What do we do now? Can you help us?"

They are all bright people, mostly successful, usually in their 60s, and they are confessing to me that they know very little about financial and legal matters. That feeling of uncertainty is quite understandable. They often operate their businesses in small towns, which have many good family businesses—a café, a hardware store, a grocery—but may have little in the way of the particular expertise needed to deal with the transition of a business. They cannot find anyone to talk to about these matters, and they feel lost.

So many families know they want to do something, and they've been talking about it at every Thanksgiving dinner for years, but they don't know the first step. They may feel their particular situation is too convoluted to solve, but there are ways to make it happen.

I have worked with many of those people whom the politicians so often praise when they point out that the small business people of our towns and our city neighborhoods are the backbone of America. After 40 years of working with hundreds of family-owned businesses across the country, I can tell you that when it comes to selling and retiring, the transition worries most of them. They are venturing into new territory, and they know they only have one chance to do it right.

A fundamental question is whether someone within the family will take over. A lot of families simply don't know that answer, even if they think they do. The conversation often goes like this:

"So do your boys want to buy the company?" I ask.

"Yes, sure they do," the proud parents respond, beaming. "They've both been working for us for years, and we're thinking they will be buying us out someday."

"Which one should become the president?"

"We don't know."

"Who's going to have the 51 percent controlling interest?"

"We don't know."

And that's okay. We're here to help people figure it all out. Sometimes I do hear, "Oh, certainly! That's all set—our daughter has been running the show for three years, and she's doing a great job. We take long vacations and don't worry about a thing." That's the idea. When I hear that, I know we're halfway home. We have a buyer, and that buyer is in the family.

But of course some owners have no children. Even when they do, I sometimes come to suspect—and the parents come to acknowledge—that maybe none of the children really has the inclination or ability to run the company. They may show up every day to stock shelves and deal with customers, but may have other aspirations for their lives that they have yet to admit to Mom and Dad.

So now what? The first step depends on the answers to a number of questions. Will the company be sold to an outsider? What is the company really worth? We need a reliable valuation for the business, no matter who is buying it. If our firm does the valuation, we can calculate taxes, cash flow, and profitability. It's like an X-ray, by which we can see into the company by looking at the last three or four years of financial statements.

One of our senior partners recently finished a valuation for some people in Alabama. There were two owners, one with 40 percent and the other with 60 percent. The latter wanted to sell his interest to the former, and he thought the company was worth $1.2 million. They agreed to call me to do the valuation, because their particular industry is one of several that we know inside and out. We speak regularly at the industry's conventions. We did the valuation, and it came in at $490,000. That result brought both of them back to reality and to the bargaining table. The 40 percent owner still wanted to take over, but he wasn't willing to pay $1.2 million.

It's important that the valuation be prepared by someone who knows the industry. Knowledge and experience with the industry help in determining what the business is really worth, the cash flow that will make the deal work, and how the taxes should be handled. It's a great starting point for any business owner when they are beginning to consider selling.

I tell people who are uncertain about how to proceed that there might be five or ten potential solutions. We talk about the options and weigh the pros and cons, and then it is up to the business owners to choose the one that best fits their family's needs. I have found it gratifying to see the moment when their eyes light up and they see for themselves the perfect solution to a question that had been stumping them. "I didn't know that was possible!" they say. "Can we do that?" I'm pleased to respond: "Yes, you can."

SIX MAJOR CONCERNS OF SUCCESSION PLANNING

In order to start drafting a succession blueprint and start putting all the pieces together, we must consider a lot of moving parts and whether the transition will be inside or outside the family. There are six areas of concern to address when drafting a succession plan.

#1—THE BUSINESS STRUCTURE

When we start analyzing a business and begin to develop a succession plan, one of the first things we look at is what kind of company the client has. There are a number of entities, including C corporations, which are the oldest type of corporations, and S corporations, a more modern form. The type of structure and business entity will influence the path we take in developing a plan.

Limited liability companies, or LLCs, have come on strong in the last 20 years or so. They exist in almost every state. Another entity is the family partnership or general partnership.

The type of company will influence how we design the blueprint to start the transition process. If you're selling outside the family, the C corporation is more complicated, because the seller will probably pay more income tax. By planning several years ahead, you can mitigate some of the taxes for a C corp. Your accountant and financial advisor, working as a team, can help you decide the best business entity for your purposes.

Does your company have voting stock and non-voting stock? When we're dealing with children, non-voting stock can sometimes be used to help equalize the estate. LLCs sometimes have preferred shares that get a 4, 5, or 6 percent dividend every year. The parents or grandparents keep those non-voting shares as a way of generating income for the older generation. The common stock, or the A stock or B stock, whatever you want to call it, would then have the growth potential. So if the company doubles in value over a period of years, it doubles in the children's name, not in the parents' name. We can structure it so that the parents or grandparents are getting income and the kids are getting the growth. The chart below illustrates most commonly used business structures:

	PARTNERSHIP	C CORPORATION	S CORPORATION	LLC
Legal Status	Separate entity from owner	Separate entity from owner	Separate entity from owner	Separate entity from owner
Separate Taxable Entity from Owner	No	Yes	Yes	Depends on tax status as sole proprietorship, partnership or corporation
Number of Owners	Unlimited	Unlimited	100	Depends on tax status as sole proprietorship, partnership or corporation
Eligible Owners	Unlimited	Unlimited	Some limitations	Depends on tax status as sole proprietorship, partnership or corporation
Owner Liability	Unlimited if general partner; limited to investment if limited partner	Limited to investment, except for personal services	Limited to investment, except for personal services	Limited to investment, except for personal services
Transferability of Ownership	Can sell all or a portion of partnership interest	Can sell all or a portion of stock	Can sell all or a portion of stock	Per articles of organization; commonly has some limitations
Allocation of Income	Based on partnership agreement if it has substantial economic reality	100% to corporation	To stockholders based on percentage of ownership	Depends on tax status as sole proprietorship, partnership or corporation
Capital Losses	Passed through to partners with normal limitations applying at partner level	Allowed only to the extent of capital gains. Any net capital loss for the year is carried back 3 tax years as short-term capital loss then forward 5 years	Passed through to shareholders with normal limitations applying at shareholder level	Depends on tax status as sole proprietorship, partnership or corporation

#2—FAMILY MEMBERS OR KEY EMPLOYEES

Besides knowing the kind of business entity you have, I want to know more about your family. I want to know about the children, including sons-in-law and daughters-in-law. Are one or two working in the business? Do they need that income? You don't want a situation in which you sell the business and the buyer immediately fires your kids.

How are the children involved? If they are not working there, could they be? Are some in a different career? What are the possibilities? We need to know how the family members fit into the process. Whether or not the children will be the buyers, business owners are often thinking about how they will be affected.

Sometimes we're working with families with three or four children, two of whom are in the business. The parents may not have thought about it, but in that case I would need to know which child would have 51 percent and which child would have 49 percent. Normally it's best to have someone in control. Between two siblings, 50/50 doesn't always work well—there can be a lot of fighting. It's usually better, over a 20- or 30-year period, if one child has 51 percent and is also the president. The other child would have 49 percent and would be vice president of operations or some other title.

This is one of the biggest stumbling blocks for families. It's tough for parents to say, "I have two kids who have been working here for 10 or 20 years, and this one gets to be president and have 51 percent, and this one will only get 49 percent and be vice president." Sometimes by talking with everybody, including the children, we can figure out who is better qualified. The children often are okay with the idea once we talk it through, and sometimes the children understand better than the parents. It might be obvious who has the ability, desire, and inclination to run the business.

We recently worked with a family in the South where four children ran the business and worked with their parents. A daughter-in-law also works in the company. The children agree that the older daughter should be president. They made their decision and are comfortable with her having that position. When the family has a game plan on who will be doing what, it's a lot easier to work through the transition.

If we're selling outside the family, the next question that I usually ask—if it's a typical small, closely held business with fewer than 30 workers—is whether a key employee or two might want to buy. A lot of owners will tell me, "My children don't want to run the business, but I have two young managers here who have been with me for ten years, and they've asked me for the chance to buy the company."

Those key employees are usually very flexible. We can design a plan in which they slowly transition into ownership over several years while the seller slowly transitions out. Neither the children nor the key employees are likely to have a big down payment when they negotiate to buy a company. We structure it over time.

We can also design it so that the owners still have their foot in the door. They still have some influence and can monitor what's happening and can slowly back away and find other things to do. If we plan for that over six or eight years, it makes it a lot easier for the owners to work their way out. It can be disconcerting when a buyer hands over a big check on a Friday afternoon, and suddenly it is retirement day. On Monday, the seller has no place to go.

#3—TRANSITION OPTIONS

There are many ways to transition a company. Parents often tell me that their sons or daughters have worked at the company for five or ten years and have done well and deserve some stock. They want to gift the children 20, 30, or 40 percent.

Gifting that stock and getting it out of the parents' names helps save estate taxes if their net worth is high. And now the son or daughter, who yesterday had no stock, all of a sudden has a significant part of the company. It drives home the fact that Mom and Dad are going to let go. Often, children tell me they doubted it would ever happen. The gifting of the stock can reenergize them.

Sometimes the parents move the stock over four years, at 10 percent per year; at the end of the fourth year, the son or daughter has 40 percent. Ordinarily, each time we gift a percentage of the company we would have to do a new valuation to find out its current worth. However, the parents could gift at both the end of December and the beginning of January—for example, in 2019–2020—and then do that again in 2021–2022. That's four years' worth of gifting with only two valuations, saving the family money. (It's also much easier and cheaper to do a valuation the second or third time. The first time is always the most time consuming.)

After the 40 percent gifting, the son or daughter could sign a promissory note and make payments to the parents for the next eight or ten years on that note. Or the child could go to a bank, borrow the money for the additional 60 percent and hand the cash to the parents. He or she would then be 100 percent owner and would make payments to the bank for the next ten years.

Some parents would prefer the lump sum; others choose the monthly payments as a good source of retirement income. If the child does go to the bank, it's a lot easier to get a loan to buy 60 percent of the company than to buy all of the company. Bankers like to see that the applicant already has 40 percent of the stock and has a proven track record of running the company well for four or five years.

During those four or five years, it's a good idea for the parents and the children to meet with the banker, talk about the business, and show him or her the tax returns. The children can talk about how they are improving sales or changing the advertising, and the banker will see the trajectory of the business and develop a comfort level that will serve the children well when they seek a loan to buy the business.

That same basic idea can be used for key employees, but it is difficult to gift to an employee. In this case, the owner would usually sell the stock to the employee but at a discount because the employee doesn't have voting control. (The children can get stock at a discount, too.) After buying discounted stock over three or four years, the key employee can either sign a note with the owner to buy the company or go to the bank for a loan. Like the children, the employee can meet with the banker at least a few times a year to develop rapport and build the banker's confidence.

When we design a transition plan, we also have to take into consideration the tax bracket of the buyer, which would be the children or the key employee, and the tax bracket of the seller. What's their ordinary income bracket, and what's the capital gains bracket? When it comes to ordinary income, a lot of the owners are going to be in the 30, 35, or 37 percent income tax bracket, while the children are probably going to be in the 22 or 24 percent bracket. For capital gains tax in 2022, the rate is 15 percent if the parents make less than

$550,000. Above that, it's 20 percent—and rises to 23.8 percent for some business owners. The sale should be structured to keep the seller in a lower bracket.

The variables that will have a huge impact are who we sell it to, how we sell it, over how many years, and which taxes are involved.

As I pointed out earlier, there are other ways to control retirement income. Sometimes Mom and Dad will be on the board of directors and get paid directors' fees. Sometimes they will sign a non-compete agreement or a consulting contract. They may even stay on the payroll and work two or three days a week. There are many ways to transition a business; we try to find two or three ways that create the least amount of tax. Reviewing those options is a major part of creating a sound transition plan.

#4—RETIREMENT SECURITY

Let's say that we know that Mom and Dad decided to gift their child 10 percent a year for four years, after which the child would sign a promissory note and buy the remaining stock, paying Mom and Dad over time. In addition to that, we need to know how much income the parents need for retirement and whether the company can afford it. During the business valuation, an estimate can be made of the usable cash flow available to buy the company stock.

If we gift a lot of the stock, the parents lose some of their future net worth. But we can make up for that by gaining income through some of those other options that I just mentioned: the directors' and consulting fees and the non-compete contract. Mom or Dad might continue to work in some capacity for the business and draw a paycheck, or we could structure a deferred compensation agreement, sometimes called a salary continuation plan. In addition, if the parents own the real estate, they would continue to receive rental income. They might also start withdrawing income from an IRA or 401(k). There are usually eight or nine ways to structure a sale to ensure that the sellers get their money, other than just one big check that would bring on a lot of tax.

The parents have to feel comfortable that the children will succeed. They often worry about what will happen if the company starts to fail under the children's guidance. That's why the attorney should always put language in the contract saying, for example, that if the new owners lose money two years in a row, the seller can buy back the stock, take back voting control, or hold the stock in escrow until the seller is paid off. There are a lot of ways to build such safeguards into the contract.

I find that sellers are surprised that the money need not come in a lump sum and that they have so many options for getting paid and maintaining the cash flow they need for retirement security. They see that they have options about how to sell, when to sell, and how to reduce taxes. They can feel secure about their retirement and reassured that the company and the employees will be protected and that the buyers will be able to succeed. Parents generally don't want to structure a deal that would compromise their children's chances of being successful business owners.

#5—TAX DECISIONS

About 20 years ago, I worked with a family in Maine in which two of the sons, who were in their 40s, had taken over the company from their father and uncle. "The payments are so high we can hardly afford it," they told me. "We have to support our own families, and we're not able to do all of this."

I asked them who had structured the deal and how. "Well, our accountant set it up this way," they explained. They said he just figured out the value of the company, which was a high number, and then structured the transition as a stock sale.

There are no tax benefits on a stock sale. So to make the payments, those young men had to earn a high income every year, pay a high income tax, and then write a monthly check to the father and uncle with the cash left after tax. Then the father and uncle had to pay the capital gains tax. Uncle Sam was the only winner.

The sons had been making payments for ten years or more, and they were struggling. They wanted to know if there was another way to do this. We helped by reducing the note by gifting some of it; the father and the uncle had not gifted any stock in the beginning, so instead we had them do just that. The note was about $300,000 each, so we gifted about $100,000 of the note to the two sons, and that reduced the size of the debt—and the amount of the payments.

Then we put the father and the uncle on as consultants. They received consulting income, which was taxable to them but deductible to the company. That saved the young men $6,000 or $7,000 a month in taxes, just by making it deductible to the company and taxable to their father and uncle. The father and uncle were in lower tax brackets. The arrangement helped both generations: the boys got a far better cash flow, and the father and uncle were assured of the continued retirement security.

That story illustrates why it can be best to bring in experts to structure the sale. You want the help of an accountant, attorney, and financial advisor who are involved in a lot of business sales and understand the tax consequences. It might seem logical to just figure out the value of a company, divide it into ten years of payments, and have the younger generation buy out the older generation in a stock sale and be done with it. But it's not that easy. There are a lot of taxes to consider.

Taxes were a lot higher when I started my career back in 1970. The rate was close to 70 percent, and for some, when you added in state, city, and county taxes, it was nearly 90 percent. Trying to structure a sale in that kind of tax bracket becomes pretty difficult. Now the maximum federal bracket is 37 percent for ordinary income, which puts a lot of people at about 45 percent with state taxes added. That's still pretty high but not like 50 years ago.

Good advisors can help you keep more of the value of your business so that it is not taxed as heavily, as we have seen in these examples of gifting and discounting and finding other streams of income in lieu of one cash payment.

Another consideration is whether the business owns the real estate. I emphasize to our clients that the real estate should never be held inside the same company as the business. An S corporation or an LLC can own the business, but the real estate should always be kept in a separate LLC or family limited partnership. Keep them as two separate entities. Never put them together.

Let's say you have a corporation that owns your business and the buildings and the real estate. You have run that company for 40 years and built up value. The business has increased in value because sales are higher, profits are higher, and inventory is higher. The real estate in that corporation has increased in value over the last 40 years, and the buildings have also increased in value and they have been depreciated on your tax return every year. Now you have decided to sell your business and move on to semi-retirement or doing something different. Does the buyer want to buy the business and the real estate or just the business? What happens to the corporation if you sell the business but keep all of the buildings?

If you have a C corporation or S corporation the taxes will be different if you sell the business along with the real estate. The C corporation will pay taxes, but if you have an S corporation all of the taxable gain will pass through to your personal tax return. By having your business in one entity and the buildings and real estate in a separate entity, your options for selling the company are much better. You have more choices, and you have the ability to control the taxes on the sale.

As you review the options, it's important to also think about whether the buyer will be able to afford what you are proposing. You need to think about the buyer's tax bracket and how the transaction would look from his or her perspective. Will the buyer have enough cash flow to succeed? If the buyer is from outside the family, it's up to the buyer to watch out for the tax consequences. But when the buyer is inside the family or a key employee, I take a particularly close look at how the deal will play out for all involved.

Again, paying the seller to become a consultant has been an effective strategy in many sales that I have negotiated. The buyer gets a tax deduction for those payments, and the seller gets the desired cash flow from the deal. That's one of a variety of tax-saving maneuvers that may help you.

#6—BUSINESS AND ESTATE DOCUMENTS

I also talk with families about the business and estate documents needed to protect the business and family. In Chapter 8, we examine these documents in detail.

For example, if the parents are gifting stock to the children, the children should sign a buy-sell agreement prepared by their attorney the same day they get their shares. That protects the company in case something happens to any of the stockholders, such as death, divorce, or disability. The parents often want to give the son or daughter a good portion of the stock, but what happens if a marriage breaks up? What if the child dies? Where does the stock go?

The way to protect the stock is through legal documents. The children sign an agreement that if some unfortunate event happens—death, divorce, disability, personal bankruptcy, termination—the company and the other stockholders control the stock. If the son were to divorce, the stock would stay with the family and would not go to the ex-spouse. If the daughter died in a car accident, the company and the family would control the stock. It wouldn't get into the hands of people outside the family.

Every stockholder also should have a will and in most cases a revocable living trust. The trust document controls the stock, and the trustee knows there's a buy-sell agreement that determines where the stock goes. Sometimes a son or daughter intends to buy the company but so far has only a fraction of the stock. He or she needs to be able to get the rest of the stock if the parents die. The buy-sell agreement can have language saying that if something happens to the parents who have majority control of the stock, then the person who has only 10 percent has the first right to buy all the stock.

Together, the buy-sell agreements, the wills, and the trusts control where the stock goes and keep it in the family. That makes the parents feel better and also makes the kids buying the company feel better. By making sure that such agreements get drafted, we help families avoid some highly unfortunate situations. I have heard of cases such as one where a son and his wife bought out the parents, and then the son died in a car accident. The ex-daughter-in-law inherited all the stock and remarried. As a result, strangers were running the company, and the parents were cut out of the business that they had wanted to stay in the family.

Business documents could also include a long-term lease on the property. Imagine a case in which the owner wants to sell the stock to a son but give the building to two daughters. The two daughters and their husbands decide that the rent for the building in which the business operates isn't high enough. The lease may only have a few more years to go, and when it expires, they double the rent.

I've seen this happen. The son either pays the higher rent or goes down the road a half-mile and builds new headquarters or rents another building. To prevent that, the lease agreement could say that the son has a new ten-year lease with a couple of five-year options upon buying the remainder of the stock. This protects him and the company. His sisters and their husbands can't throw him out.

Those are a few examples of the legal documents that are needed as a business owner anticipates selling the business. The legal documents basically do what Mom and Dad would have done if they were still alive and had voting control. You can have all the greatest ideas for transitioning and saving on taxes, but without the proper documents, your plan could backfire. Unfortunately, a handshake doesn't work anymore.

WHY OWNERS AVOID PLANNING TO SELL

Sometimes the owners lack a good candidate to take over the business, so they keep putting it off. If neither a key employee nor the children want the company, finding a buyer can be difficult. In bigger cities, you might be able to find a competitor who is interested in buying your company. Maybe they want a second, third, or fourth store. But most of those 34 million businesses are in smaller towns. If no one in the family or inside the company wants to buy it, the owners just keep on going, working year after year. Some like it that way—they want to die with their boots on—but many really want to retire.

Nowadays, a lot of businesses belong to either a buying cooperative organization or a franchise. If you have a McDonald's franchise, maybe the McDonald's people will help you find a buyer. Or if you have a retail hardware or floor-covering store, the cooperative might help you find a buyer. Even if you're in the middle of Wyoming or Montana, there might be somebody within 100 miles who would like to buy your company. The various co-ops and franchises, of which there are thousands in the United States, are starting to help sellers find buyers.

Another reason that people put off retiring is that they simply cannot afford to do it. A lot of business owners pump their profit every year right back into the company—buying more inventory, more shelving, more equipment—or hire another person. Because of that, they haven't developed a high net worth outside of the business.

If it's a small store in a small town, it's difficult for me to help them sell it at a price high enough so that they have money left over after taxes to retire. They realize they have nothing else to fall back on, so they know they have to keep working.

These are some of the reasons that people don't sell: They don't have a buyer, they don't want to quit, or they can't afford to quit because they haven't developed a high enough net worth outside the business. People often get conflicting advice which complicates their decision-making. They tell me, "We've been talking to our attorney, and he said one thing. And then we talked to our accountant, and he had a different idea. And we talked to our insurance agent, stockbroker, and banker, too—and they all had different things to say."

Business owners get confused, because they think that all of these people who they may have known a long time are good advisors, when actually none of them are experts at business transitions. The business owner doesn't know who's right and who's wrong or which way to jump and so winds up doing nothing.

CHAPTER
TWO

GETTING AN
EARLY START

I worked with a family where a father was selling to his son, and we developed a detailed ten-year time line. Every year along that time line, each could see his particular responsibilities. Initially, the father would run all the company meetings and do all the hiring and firing, and he would work with the bankers, attorneys, and accountants on the taxes.

The son would also be attending those meetings, and after a few years he would start running them and the father would back away. The father might attend or perhaps not—on the time line, he is doing less and less. After eight or nine years, the son is running everything.

He does all the hiring, all the firing. Everybody works for him. The father just shows up once in a while.

Over the ten-year period, the company has a smooth transition. A ten-year plan—or an eight-year plan or a five-year plan—is always better than even a one-year plan. Planning ahead for what will happen every year during your time line is much better than having no plan at all. You need to get an early start—I usually tell people at least three to five years, and sometimes ten years ahead of time, is a good idea.

If you want to sell but don't have a prospect in the hopper, don't panic. You still need to start planning for the company as though you had a buyer. You want the company to look good, and you want to start developing higher profitability and lower expenses. You want to start cleaning up the building. You might want to add on to the buildings, offices, or showrooms or buy more equipment, vehicles, or whatever enhances your business. Over the next five or six years, you want to develop the company to the point where, at the end of the line, it looks perfect. It has the best financial statements. It has the best tax returns. It has the best-trained employees.

FIRST STEPS

To start developing a plan, you need first to choose your advisors. Business owners should continue to do what they do best and let others do what they do best—that is, help analyze the situation. In Chapter 10, we look at just who should be on your "dream team" of advisors.

Initially get them all together for a two-hour meeting and then 6 or 12 months later have another two-hour meeting. Tell them how the company is doing, and ask about any new tax laws. Do they have any new ideas that could help in your situation? Pick their brains to start developing your blueprint. Be sure to meet with those advisors at least a couple of hours every year to keep them updated on your situation.

Selling to someone who already has a company within your industry will normally get you the highest price. If you know that you will be selling the company to someone in your industry because your kids and employees don't want it, then over the next several years you need to be running the company knowing that you're going to sell it to an outsider.

It doesn't make sense, for example, to hire an in-house controller if in three years you're going to be selling the business to somebody who already has a controller. Why put someone on your payroll for only three years? Instead, for the next three years you might pay your accounting firm to do some extra work for you.

If the buyer will be a family member, then make sure that during the next one or two years he or she is thoroughly trained. The children need to work at the company for at least two or three years, preferably five or ten.

About a year ago, I met with a couple who told me that the key manager wanted to buy their company, as did their son, a new college graduate who had just joined the company. The two of them intended to work together, and the couple was ready to agree to the plan. I suggested that they let the two buyers work together for a year to see how they got along and whether they could decide who would be in charge. A year later, the couple told me the two were getting along fine. Now we're starting the process of the sale, and it has worked out well. The key employee understands that the son is blood and he's not, and the owners are trying to decide the percentages of ownership. The young buyers are okay with that arrangement.

As you prepare during your time line, remember to gradually start backing away if you are going to be selling to the children or to a key employee. You can scream and yell like Vince Lombardi all you want from the sidelines, but you have to hold back from stepping out on the field. It's like being on a board of directors. If the parent becomes chairman of the board and the child becomes president, the chairman can yell at the board meetings but can't walk into the company and start firing people. He or she has to back away and let the son or daughter call the shots, without reversing them. Otherwise, the child will feel demoralized.

LATER STEPS

In the second half of your succession planning process, you're getting closer to crunch time. Let's say you have a four-year plan. In the first two years, you were doing the background things that we discussed. Now, with two years to go before you would like to sell, it's time to really get things looking good.

You need to think differently than perhaps you have in 30 years. Your approach needs to center on making the company look as attractive as possible in the eyes of the buyer.

FINANCIAL CLEANUP

You likely need to clean up all the corporate financials. Having looked at hundreds and hundreds of financial statements, I have seen that owners often have 30 years of accumulated assets and liabilities that they have left on the financial statement. They haven't worried about taking them off or making the statement look better because nobody sees it except them.

As you prepare to sell, particularly to an outsider, you want to make the last two to three years of financial statements look as good as possible. You want to show your company in the best light.

For example, if I see "loan to shareholder" on a financial statement, my first question is, why? Why did the company lend money to the shareholder? There might have been tax reasons, but we need to get that off of the statement if we can. The buyer is going to see that and ask questions.

Also, there might be a loan on the corporate financial statement, where it says "loan from shareholder." There may be good reasons for the loan, but you want to have your answer ready and clear. Did you lend the money to the company because it was losing money and desperately needed cash, or was it done for some other reason? If it doesn't need to be on there and if you don't need that shareholder loan, then get it off.

Another example: Perhaps three years ago you bought a truck and got a 12 percent rate on a loan for it. A buyer might ask why the bank charged such a high interest rate and wonder if something was wrong with the company at that time. If you have any high interest rate loans, refinance them and get them down to today's level.

Start going through that financial statement. Look at every line item and make each one look good, lean, and competitive. It's sort of like shaving and putting on a good suit before you go on a date. You want to make the best first impression when you're selling this company. Don't give anyone cause for concern. Stop the questions before they are asked.

A buyer will be looking at everything you were doing in the last two or three years before selling the company. They will want to see the financial statements, the tax returns, and the loan negotiations with the bank. If the bank is lending you a lot of money at a low interest rate, that means a lot to the buyer, because it indicates the bank thinks you have a good company.

As you get closer to the date when you would like to sell, it is also important to improve the usable cash flow and profits. If your children or key employees are buying the business, they need a lot of cash flow to pay you over time. If the buyer will be somebody in the industry outside the family, then the higher the "EBITDA," or cash flow, the higher the sales price.

EBITDA, a term used by accountants and valuation experts, stands for "Earnings Before Interest, Taxes, Depreciation, and Amortization." I usually call it usable cash flow. In the last two or three years of ownership, there's absolutely no reason not to build up your usable cash flow.

If I look at a business' tax return for the previous year and it had $100,000 of corporate profit on which it paid tax, then we add several items to arrive at the EBITDA. Let's say there's a depreciation of $40,000, so we add that back. Now it's $140,000. There was $20,000 of interest paid on loans. Now it's $160,000. Then the owner spent $10,000 traveling across the country going to conventions for his industry, so now it's $170,000. Then the company bought his pickup truck or his car and paid for his gas. Now it's $190,000. The company also paid for other benefits, maybe health insurance. Now it's $200,000.

That means the usable cash flow is not just $100,000 but closer to $200,000. When you sell this business, you are selling a business that really has $200,000 of cash flow for the buyer to work with, not $100,000. I want that EBITDA number, after the add-backs, to be as big as possible. The higher that number is, the more valuable the business will be.

You want to make certain that figure is as high as possible during the last two or three years because the buyer will be looking at that. Part of that $200,000 can be used by your son or daughter to pay you over time. Or if they go to the bank and borrow money, they need that $200,000 of cash flow to help pay the bank loan. A key manager likewise will need that cash flow to pay the bank.

PERSONNEL CLEANUP

In the last two years before you sell the company, you also have to start taking a hard look at your people and your payroll costs.

I work with a lot of industries in which the expense for the owner's salary is about 4 percent of sales. All the other employees added together would be a payroll expense of about 18 percent of total sales. That's a total of 22 percent. Industries with a higher gross margin, like 45 or 50 percent, can have a slightly higher payroll. Industries with a lower gross margin, of perhaps 25 percent, cannot afford that.

Normally, payroll and benefits are the owner's biggest expenses that suck profit out of the company. Keep payroll and other expenses close to industry averages. I see a lot of companies where it should be 20 percent but is actually 22 or 24 percent. Those four percentage points of sales amount to the year's profit for most businesses. If that describes you, that means your people are getting paid higher than the industry average but you are making nothing on the bottom line.

I recently worked with a family where the total payroll was 31 percent of sales. "I don't understand why I'm not making any money," the owner told me.

"Well, right here is all your money, in that 31 percent. You've got good people but about four or five too many of them."

"Yes, but they're good friends. I like them. I don't want to fire them."

"Okay, then you're not going to sell your company for much money. It's not worth much. You're not making much profit."

In the last two or three years of their succession planning process, owners have to get serious about protecting their family and their future. The payroll and occupancy costs are the biggest expenses for most retail-type companies.

Start hiring and firing people. Get the right people in the right position. The buyer will first talk about price, and then the very next question will be, "Tell me about your people."

One business owner I worked with was 78 years old and had two key store managers, both of whom were 70. A buyer would expect to have to replace those two managers soon and to train replacements. It is important to make sure your workforce is attractive to a buyer, with the right training and credentials. If the buyer doesn't have to spend a lot of money on hiring more people, then maybe they will pay more for the business.

FACILITY CLEANUP

In the 6 to 12 months before selling the business, start working on the facility. Start painting the walls and making sure all the shelving looks good. If a forklift backed into a wall five years ago, fix the dent in the wall. Get things cleaned up. Clean the floors. A shabby appearance will reflect poorly on the owner and the employees. Start cleaning everything up inside and outside.

The buyer is going to drive by your building at night. If there's a lighted sign that's supposed to say "Smith Air Conditioning" but instead says "h Air oning," that's a problem. You want to look good by day and also by night.

If a potential buyer sees that you care about maintenance, that you have good employees in place, and that your profit is good, then there is little to argue about. So clean up. Clean up your financial statements, clean up your personnel, clean up your facilities. You want to be sitting pretty.

CHAPTER THREE

MAXIMIZING VALUE

Several years ago, I worked with two sisters and a brother on the East Coast who had bought out their parents a couple of decades earlier. The siblings were getting to the point, in their late 50s, where they wanted to sell the business. We did a valuation. When it came back, one of the daughters let me know how disappointed she was.

"I've been here 20 years," she said. "I really thought it would be worth more money."

I tried to explain to her that time has nothing to do with company value. "You could work here for another 20 years, and that wouldn't mean it would be worth more," I said.

All that time, the siblings had been milking the company of every dollar in profit. They each took high incomes, and they didn't reinvest anything. The company had almost zero stockholders' equity. Very few employees would remain if the owners sold and walked away. It had no built-up value.

"You can't suck a company dry every year and expect it to go up in value," I said. "You have to reinvest. You have to do things year after year and make the right business decisions, not just put in your time."

She thought every year her business should go up in value just because she'd been working at it. Businesses need long-term planning to improve their stockholders' equity and usable cash flow.

Think of it this way: You can live in a house for 20 years, but if you don't fix the windows, the carpet, and the roof, then the house is going to go down in value. Just because you live there doesn't mean it's worth more.

It's the same with a business. You've got to put money back in it if you want to get money out later. If you have no other resources and you have neglected the upkeep of your business, you may not be able to sell it for what you need to have sufficient income for retirement. People in that situation may feel they have to work forever.

ATTENDING TO THE BALANCE SHEET

As you look to maximize your company's value, you want to consider every line item on the balance sheet. How much capital do you need? If you're using a high line of credit and borrowing a lot of money every year, then you should probably consider putting more cash back into the company. Take some of your profits and put them back in so that you borrow less money.

When I look at financial statements and see that the company's line of credit has increased every year for five years, I conclude that it doesn't have enough capital. The company is borrowing more and more money to keep going. Somewhere down the road, it will hit a brick wall. One of these days, whether in three years or five, the owner will walk into the bank and say, "I need to increase my line of credit," and the bank will say, "No, we're not going to do it. You don't have enough profit. You don't have a good enough track record to increase your line of credit."

Before the bank says no, start putting some capital back into the business. Don't increase your line of credit every year. Look at how much capital you need and how much debt you need. Some debt is okay. Especially with the low interest rates as of 2021, companies can borrow money at 3 to 7 percent. Those are good interest rates. If I can borrow at 6 percent to buy inventory that I can mark up 40 percent, I don't mind netting those 34 points. Borrowing a little money, especially in low interest rate environments, is not a bad idea. Just don't let the debt turn around and bite you.

Don't be dependent on the bank line of credit. A lot of business owners learned that the hard way during the recession of 2008–2009. Many probably experienced it also back in the 1990s and the 1980s. In a recession, banks have to cut back on loans. You don't want to be at the bank's mercy. You want to be strong financially.

Look at your balance sheet. Look at the capital. Look at the debt. There's an old saying, "Cash is king," and it's true. It was true 40 years ago, and it's still true today. Remember that. More capital and less debt is a good idea.

LOCATION, INVENTORY, SERVICE

The location of your business plays a major role in its value. Some businesses require retail traffic and need to be on Main Street. Some wholesale companies can be blocks away from Main Street. Some people can be on the edge of town. Whatever business you're in, you want the most suitable location.

If you have a half-million square feet of warehouse space, you probably want to be within a few blocks of the interstate. You don't want your truck drivers driving five or ten miles through stoplights. Whether you need warehousing or retail space, the location matters. In one way or another, it will help to drive sales, which drives profitability.

The quality of your inventory also has a lot to do with your company's value. You need to monitor your inventory constantly and keep it fresh and up to date. If you have a store with the latest goods, people will notice and come in to shop—and increase your profit. That increases the value of the company.

You also maximize profit by offering excellent customer service. Train your employees well. If you are associated with a purchasing cooperative, find out about the training programs it offers. Franchises also have a variety of programs to train employees on how to treat customers. Customer service is highly important in today's world.

Spend the necessary money on the right kind of advertising, and pay attention to the ever-increasing tendency of customers to shop online. Many businesses have a website and online inventory. Online shopping has become an essential part of retailing. Businesses need to spend what it takes to reach the right people, whether it's through newspaper fliers or digital marketing.

WATCH THAT MARGIN

As you seek ways to maximize the value of your business, you need to pay close attention to your gross margin. Some store owners will go two or three years without adjusting the margins. That's a mistake. You should be watching your margins monthly, even weekly. You might say, generally, "I can make money at 38 percent gross margin"—and that's nice, but it may need to be at 40 percent on that particular electrical item or on that pair of shoes or on those industrial tools.

You need to price everything competitively with your industry. You don't want to be 1 or 2 percent low. Set the price right to generate more money. You need to be able to show that you are right with the industry standards or better. That's what a valuation company will examine when determining what your business is worth.

You must not be off in any category—whether it's gross margin on any of the items that you sell or your payroll, rent, or expenses. For example, retail companies spend a lot of money on bank charges. When a customer uses a credit card, the store has to pay 1 or 1.5 percent to the credit card company. If you're paying 2.2 percent, the question becomes why you haven't negotiated a lower rate. It's an example of an expense that might easily be trimmed. You want to get your expenses down to rock bottom so that you can show more profit, which makes your company more valuable.

NEGOTIATING THE PRICE

If you are selling to your children or to a key employee, you are likely to take a somewhat different view on maximizing the value of your business. You probably are not going to push for the absolute highest price as you might if you were selling to an outside buyer.

Again, the valuation appraisers normally look at a three- or five-year average income. Let's say the valuation reports, looking at the three-year average income, comes out at $500,000—even though it might be $550,000 if it were just the last two years or $600,000 if it were just the last year. The valuation will also be influenced by the price for which similar businesses recently have sold in your industry—much the way an appraiser values a house based on recent comparable sales.

The valuation is just the starting point, however. If you get a three-year valuation at $500,000 for your company, the business might be worth $550,000 or $575,000 to an outside buyer, so you would start negotiating from the higher price. If you are dealing with someone inside the family, it might be worth less money.

An outside buyer within the industry is also likely to already have back office personnel to handle accounting and financial work. Such a buyer, therefore, would immediately let a few people go. Let's say the buyer would not need two of your employees who were making $40,000 a year. That's $80,000 of additional cash flow. Knowing that, the buyer often is willing to pay more for the company.

A buyer inside the family, however, would not see it that way. Those back office people would need to stay, so the additional cash flow would not be generated. Therefore, the perceived value of the company would be less. That's an example of a factor that plays into the negotiations for maximum value. It depends on who the buyer is.

ALL THE RIGHT MOVES

To maximize the value of your business, I cannot emphasize enough the importance of having excellent corporate attorneys who have been involved in selling hundreds of companies. They will handle documents such as the letter of intent to sell or the term sheet, and they will also work with you on representations and warranties. You need to take great care with those documents, as I explain in Chapter 8.

With the reps and warranties, you are making guarantees regarding conditions. For example, you might represent that you repaired the roof three years ago and there are no leaks. Or that you didn't bury 50 batteries in the back parking lot, that you haven't been dumping paint down the drain, or that there's no asbestos in the building. Sellers may be required to make many kinds of guarantees to buyers. If the buyer finds that a condition is not as you represented, you will be responsible. Perhaps you forgot about something you did 20 years ago, but if it becomes a problem, the buyer will want some money back.

A seller who is only going to go through this once will not want to spend a lot of money on legal fees. Quite often we let the buyer's attorney prepare the documents. Then the seller's attorneys can go through them, cutting out or rewording a sentence or paragraph. It is generally easier and cheaper to review and revise than it is to draft, although sometimes we may want the seller's attorney to prepare the documents, then the buyer's attorneys can refine the wording. It may sound like a game, but it's a very important one. It's a game of semantics. The wording is crucial.

A lawyer who has been through this hundreds of times will protect you by watching out for appropriate wording in all the legal documents. The old saying is, "The job is not done until the paperwork is completed." This is where accountants and attorneys earn their fees, making sure you're paying the least amount of tax and that the legal documents are worded to protect you. All of that goes into maximizing the value of the sale.

The cost of a good attorney is usually money well spent. When the buyers and the sellers all get together with their representatives, I find myself looking around the room, trying to size everyone up. It can feel like a game of chess—all the right moves, with all the right players. That small-town lawyer you've known for 30 years will not be able to thoroughly analyze documents that some big law firm has prepared. I mean no disrespect by that. He's probably very smart, but he's a generalist. He should be there with you, but at this point you need a specialist. For this particular operation, you need a heart surgeon.

At the end of the first meeting, when the buyer and his team head to the elevator, I want his lawyers to be saying to him: "Those guys have some good counsel. We're going to have to sharpen our pencils on this one. This is not going to be a cakewalk."

WANT AN EXTRA MILLION?

A lot of business owners, when they are thinking about selling, have been running the company rather casually for many years. It's time for a change. In the three years before the sale, I suggest trying to increase gross margins by 1 percent per year. There are many ways to increase the gross margin that much.

Also, try to reduce expenses by 2 percent per year. You ought to be able to cut down on use of paper or paperclips. And what about pay raises—are a lot of your employees already at the maximum pay for their positions? There are bound to be places that you can cut 2 percent of your expenses per year while at the same time trying to increase gross margins by 1 percent.

If you can work on that for the next 36 months, you'll greatly increase the value of your business. Those three points, when dropped to the bottom line, can probably increase the value of your company at least 20 or 30 percent. You can gain a huge amount of leverage that way. Once they see the benefit, a lot of business owners somehow find creative ways to make those cuts and adjust the margin. It's like telling them, "How would you like to have an extra million dollars in your pocket in a few years?"

In all those years when the company was making a profit, you might not have worried too much about expenses. But $500 here and $1,000 there add up pretty fast. In your final three years of business, you need to start cutting out some of the waste and increasing some of the prices. Can you get an extra 1 percent? Yes, probably. Your competitors are 2 percent higher, so you can increase your price 1 percent. Go for it. It's all going to drop into your pocket. You'll make more money the next three years, and you'll sell the company for a higher price. You get two benefits.

Look at the financials. Look at the cash flow, costs, and margins. They are highly important, particularly in those final years before the sale. Along with the negotiations and the preparation of the documents, it all goes into maximizing the value of your business.

CHAPTER FOUR

RETIREMENT INCOME SECURITY

Two sisters bought the company from their father and have run it for many years. They reinvested in it, made it grow bigger and bigger, and eventually reached the point where they wanted to retire. But, like so many business owners, they didn't know how to sell it, when to sell it, or how much to ask.

I have worked with the sisters for a long time on a variety of estate planning and other family issues. When they were in their late 60s and began talking about retirement, we did a valuation to show them the amount that they probably could get for their business — a few million dollars.

It wasn't enough. We did our best to cut down on the taxes, but the business was a C corporation, which makes it harder to do that. After taxes, the sisters would not have the money necessary for retirement. They both made high salaries, enjoyed a good lifestyle, and had nice homes. But they didn't save a lot. They did not attend to all the building blocks necessary for an adequate retirement income.

Faced with the facts, they decided not to sell the company, because they did not want to reduce their income by about 50 percent. So they continue to run the company, year after year, earning those high salaries for as long as they are able. They have their income for now—but they haven't arranged to have an income for life.

It's not as if they have to labor long hours. In this case, the sisters have three or four good key employees who do most of the work, so one sister puts in 10 or 15 hours a week and the other even less. They are desperate to keep those key people. If they lose them, they're out of luck—neither sister would be able to put in 30 or 40 hours a week, and it would be difficult to find somebody to run a business with 30 or 40 employees that grosses several million a year in sales. You just can't hire somebody off the street to do that.

As it stands, the company is doing okay, but it could be doing better. To maintain their good salaries, the sisters are not reinvesting in the company as they did in previous decades. That is bound to hurt any business after several years. You have to maintain the premises and modernize if you want customers to keep coming in the door.

So even though the sisters are able to maintain their lifestyle, they are in treacherous waters. So much could go wrong. A ruthless competitor might see the handwriting on the wall, open up a modern shop nearby, and crush them within a few years. I am continuing to work with them and with their key employees to make the best of the situation, but this is a lesson for all business owners. This scenario is not rare. Many owners are likewise vulnerable, as they keep working without any real hope for retirement. And it need not be that way.

THE NEED TO DIVERSIFY

In this chapter, we look at what business owners need to do to diversify and build their net worth so that they can attain retirement income security. All around the country, a lot of 70- and 80-year-olds are still running the company. They have little choice. Like the sisters, they have to hang onto the company so that they can keep that salary coming in. Their net worth is primarily that one big asset, the business, and in the years that they have operated it, they have failed to diversify.

In cases where the children intend to buy the business, there are a few more options for developing an income for life. When selling outside the family, however, those options are more limited, particularly when the owners have not acted to protect their net worth and have little in the way of additional resources.

Some owners have been smart and successful business people. They may run a grocery, a paint store, a shoe shop, or a hardware store. It seems everyone in town knows them by name. They have done very well for the employees and for their families. Their kids finished college and went on to other careers. Their families, employees, and community appreciate all that they have done. But now, at the peak of their career when they should be able to walk away to go fly fishing or whatever they choose to do, they feel forced to keep the company going.

WHAT'S BEST
FOR ALL CONCERNED

When you're thinking about selling the company and developing a long-term income stream, you want to think about what's best for the business and what's best for you and for your family.

In my nearly four decades of working with families, I have learned that about 20 to 25 percent of business owners will sell to one or more of their children. About 15 to 20 percent will sell to key employees because the children chose a different career and don't want to own the company. And about 50 to 60 percent will sell to somebody else in the industry: an independent grocery store will sell to another grocery store, a lumberyard will sell to a lumberyard, and a manufacturing company will sell to a manufacturing company. The remaining businesses will just close their doors.

If you expect to sell to someone in the industry, look around at your competitors to see who might be interested. Most business people are aware of who might want to buy. They may even have shared ideas at conventions. In a bigger metropolitan area, it's usually—though not always—easier to find a buyer. Typically, in Texas, Wyoming, or Montana, we may have to go a hundred miles to find a competitor who might want to buy—although in those states, driving that distance isn't a big deal.

And so, depending on circumstances, you may sell to your children, to your key employees, or to somebody else. You want to be thinking about that three to five years ahead of time, because your strategy, and your retirement income, will depend on it. All such decisions depend, of course, on what's going on in the family—who is inclined to do what, and who, if anyone, in the family might want to be a buyer.

Sometimes the children are not the best choice to run the company. They don't want to be in the business, or they aren't capable. Even if the children are working in the business, the owners may sell to an outside buyer. In such cases, we may try to get those children a two- or three-year, no-cut employment contract. That gives the children more time to develop their skills and work with the buyer, perhaps getting promoted and staying for a long time.

In any case, all business owners want to maintain their net worth. You haven't worked 30 or 40 years just to sell the company and find your net worth cut in half. You need the highest reasonable net worth so that you can retire comfortably. If you must pay out $100,000 or $500,000 in income taxes or long-term capital gains taxes when you sell the business, that's going to reduce your net worth, so what can we do to help build it back up?

As we discussed earlier, that income need not result directly from the sale proceeds. Parents often gift stock to their children to help with the transaction and then collect rent on the real estate, or they take a consulting contract for ten years, or get paid to serve on the board of directors. That gives the parents income and also puts them in a role of coach, which the children may need. Wisdom is an asset.

However, it's important to design the sale to also protect the company and the employees. If the buyers—whether the children or key employees—agree to such a high price that they can't afford the payments, they could go out of business, and then all the employees would lose their jobs. The deal needs to be good for the seller, the buyer, the company, and the employees. It has to work. If the company goes under, your years of hard work are lost. When devising a strategy to maximize retirement income and minimize taxes, it's important to find the right balance between seller and buyer, particularly when the transaction is within the family or involves key employees.

We can't strip the company of all of its cash. After taxes, there needs to be enough cash flow that the buyer can afford the payments to the seller and also make some profit, with enough left over to reinvest in the business. A company's cash flow is like gas for a car: if it runs out, it won't go. Don't starve the company of all the cash, because you're just hurting yourself in the long run.

WHO GETS THE TAX BREAKS?

How much money the sellers will net from the deal—and how much they will have available for retirement income security—is influenced largely by taxes. We need to know the tax brackets for all involved in the transaction. We need to figure in the federal, state, and local levies. Is the parents' income tax bracket at 30, 35, or 37 percent? What is the kids' bracket? If the company is a C corporation, what's the tax for the C corp? Is it 21 percent? We need to know those tax brackets so that we can design the transaction to distribute the income optimally.

It's quite common that the sellers, when all the taxes are added up, are at 45 percent or more. In that case, if the children are in the 20 percent tax bracket we might be able to give them more income so that they can buy stock from the parents. Then instead of the parents paying 45 percent of all the money that they get from the sale, they might only pay long-term capital gains of 15 or 20 percent.

Let's say a son is going to buy the stock and will pay his father $10,000 a month. In order for him to afford that, the company would need to pay him about $15,000 a month on top of his regular salary so that he will net, after taxes, the additional money to make the payment. (He would probably be in about the 35 percent tax bracket.) The son hands over that $10,000 to the parent—who then pays 20 percent capital gains tax on the transaction. The son then pays maybe 35 percent, the parents pay 20 percent or more, and Uncle Sam rakes in 55 percent on the deal. Is there a better way?

When I explain it that way to audiences, I notice that everyone sits up and starts scribbling notes furiously. It's just a simple transaction, but people don't think about how much Uncle Sam eventually gets of every additional dollar the son has to earn in salary to afford the payment to the parent.

THE BUILDING BLOCKS OF RETIREMENT SECURITY

Many business owners have four of what I call building blocks for retirement security: (1) real estate, (2) retirement accounts, (3) outside investments, and (4) the value of the business itself.

It's helpful to start thinking about retirement income security when you are 30 or 40 years old and to start developing assets in these four blocks. Although it's important to keep the company up to date and current by reinvesting money into it, for your own family's protection you need to diversify and have assets in all of those four building blocks, not just one. If you are 40 years old today, and you intend to retire or sell the business at age 65, you have 25 years to start building up assets in each of these four building blocks.

#1—REAL ESTATE

It depends on the industry, but I would say about half of entrepreneurs own their real estate. Maybe they're in a strip shopping center and wind up buying the whole shopping center. Maybe they have built a standalone building for their company. Maybe it's a warehouse or a lumberyard. They own the land, and they own the building. A lot of them own the real estate personally with their spouse. Those who are more experienced put it into a limited liability company, or LLC. It's never a good idea to put the real estate inside the business. The real estate should be kept in a separate company.

If the sellers own the real estate, they can sell the company but keep the property and receive rental income in retirement. By the time they sell the company, most have either paid off the mortgage or are very close to doing so. The mortgage payment might be $4,000 a month, but they might get $8,000 a month in rent. That $4,000 difference is extra income. They might also be able to refinance and get a lower mortgage payment.

In those cases we make sure that the seller has a ten-year triple net lease. A triple net lease means that the business continues to pay for all the maintenance, all the insurance on the building, and all the real estate taxes. The new owner of the business sends the rent check to the seller or to the LLC. The seller does not have to pay the real estate taxes or the various insurance premiums. If a pothole forms in the parking lot, the new owner is the one who takes care of it and any other maintenance. The triple net lease is common in the real estate industry.

Real estate, then, is building block number one. If you own it, it can provide income for you and your spouse. Or you could give that real estate in your will or trust to children who are not in the business, thereby providing income to them, too.

#2—RETIREMENT ACCOUNTS

The second building block is a qualified retirement account, such as a 401(k) or IRA. Earlier generations had pensions. In the past, if you worked for a company for 30 years, you could retire and get a pension and health insurance for the rest of your life. Those pension plans are mostly nonexistent. Starting in the 1980s, companies began to transition to 401(k) retirement plans. Today, almost every industry big and small has developed these tax-deferred plans to which employees contribute, often with a match from the employer.

Unfortunately, I don't think that anyone who is 35 or 40 years old and starts putting money into a typical 401(k) plan can accumulate enough money in the next 20 years to retire. You just can't put enough money away. But it is a way to build retirement assets, and it is tax deductible, so I recommend taking advantage of such a plan. Others may have what's called a SIMPLE IRA, or they might have a self-employment plan, or SEP. Continue to put away as much as you can in those accounts every year. You probably cannot accumulate enough to fund your retirement, but they are a solid building block. Take advantage of the tax deductions.

Don't try to hit a home run with your retirement account. Invest it in a balanced, conservative way, and let it grow slowly. You get that big benefit up front: a tax deduction for the amount that you contribute. Most 401(k)s let you choose from 20 or 30 mutual funds. Invest in the conservative ones so that you won't lose much when the stock market takes a dive, which it inevitably will do. You don't want to have a million dollars in your 401(k) plan at age 65, as you plan to retire, and then see a plunge in the market that reduces that to $600,000. It can take several years to recover from that, and you don't have that much time.

Although you shouldn't be too aggressive with your investments in those retirement accounts, you should contribute the maximum every year. The fees and expenses are relatively high, but you cannot control those. Don't let that deter you from adding money regularly.

Be sure that you keep track of not only your investments but also the beneficiaries that you list on those accounts. In working with clients, I have often looked at their retirement plans and found, to their great surprise, that the beneficiary is an ex-spouse, and that's a disaster waiting to happen. It is essential that every few years you review the primary beneficiary as well as the contingent beneficiaries.

#3—INVESTMENTS OUTSIDE THE BUSINESS

The third building block for retirement security—liquid investments outside the company—is where most people fall short. You need that diversification—as the story about the two sisters that opened this chapter illustrated.

With some of your income, bonuses, or dividends—however you take the money out—open an investment account. I encourage people to use a discount broker rather than a full-service broker. Open an account and start buying some good, diversified assets. Buy blue chip stocks in big companies. Buy municipal bonds paying tax-free interest. With the help of your financial advisor, develop a portfolio of liquid assets. The business is illiquid. The real estate is illiquid. The home is illiquid. So add some large company stocks like Apple, Proctor & Gamble, Caterpillar, or John Deere. These types of investments are more liquid and have the additional benefit of paying dividends and add additional diversification to your investment portfolio. We discuss this more in Chapter 9.

Buying illiquid assets such as real estate would not be my first choice. For a few years, build up some liquid assets that could be sold within a day or two, like stocks and bonds. Then you might consider buying a strip shopping center, office building, apartment building, or farmland—something that you want to own that is away from the business.

Make sure, however, that your portfolio maintains liquid. In a couple of years, if the company needs a $100,000 line of credit, maybe take some of those liquid assets and lend money back to the business without going to a bank. A lot of people don't want to go to the bank to borrow money. With all that liquidity, you can become the banker—but just make sure you get paid back.

In your investment account at a discount broker, always try to minimize the expenses. Be very careful about what you're buying. Try to avoid commissions. If you buy a mutual fund or an ETF (exchange-traded fund), which are baskets of stocks, you will have some management expense. If you buy something from an insurance company, you're going to have a lot of expense because many people are getting paid. These options are good for some people but not for everyone. Understand the total expenses.

I usually tell people that 1 to 1.5 percent is normal as a management fee. However, if you are dealing with an insurance product, you're paying 2 to 4 percent every year, because with those bigger companies come bigger expenses. As you develop your liquidity, keep the expenses as low as possible, because at 3 or 4 percent a year in expenses, you lose a lot of your profits.

Properly diversifying and controlling expenses are important aspects of effective investment. A good financial advisor can help the business owner make the right decisions to develop a secure income for retirement. We go into more detail on advisors in Chapter 10.

#4—SELLING THE COMPANY

The fourth building block for retirement security is selling the company for as much as you can get. If you don't own the real estate and you don't have personal investment assets someplace else, then most of your net worth is wrapped up in your company. In order to have enough retirement income you have no choice but to sell it for as high a price as possible.

We look at a variety of factors to enhance income when selling the business. I have already mentioned a number of these. We can get as much as possible for the stock or assets of the company. We can arrange for a consulting fee. We may get some value for goodwill. Goodwill is based on the length of time that your company has been in business and the consistent profitability over the last several years. Director's fees are a possibility, especially when selling to the children or key employees, who may want the owner to stay on as a director for three to five years or longer. Deferred compensation is another common approach: the company continues to pay the owner for having run the business over the past 30 or 40 years.

Or, again, the buyer might pay rent on the real estate. A lot of people can't buy the business and the real estate at the same time, and so they buy the business and we build into the lease agreement an option to buy the real estate after several years. That way the seller will continue to get rent for at least that time.

There are other approaches, but those are the most common ones, and we have to figure out which combination of two or three ideas will work best. It all has to come together for the sellers. Before moving forward with a sale, they have to know that their net worth and their future will be secure.

CHAPTER FIVE

THE NEXT GENERATION

We recently worked with a family on the East Coast that was transitioning their company from the sixth generation to the seventh, which is quite an accomplishment. It's nice when we can keep the company going for another generation or two. Statistics show that only 30 percent of family businesses make it to the second generation; only 15 percent make it to the third generation; and only 1 or 2 percent make it to the fourth. The problem is not typically financial—bad financial decisions only destroy about 10 percent of family businesses. Usually it's a lack of trust, communication, and education.

The 100 oldest companies in the United States that are still doing business were founded between 1630 and 1850. Of those, 54 are in the original 13 colonies, and 21 were founded before 1776. The owners are families that have figured out how to keep a company going for a century or two, but most families don't come close.

Communication and education are key. I have often been asked to teach classes designed for the next generation to pass on ideas to young leaders. I hear questions such as this: "How can I get Dad to retire so I can start running this place?"

This is where a succession plan is really important. You need a multi-year plan and procedures to follow every year. As the owner, you ran the show for 30 or 40 years. You were the quarterback, calling all the plays. That won't be the case for another 30 or 40 years—and so now is the time for you to become the coach. Slowly, over the course of a few years, you'll move to the sidelines. Let somebody else throw the ball for a change and take the hits. Your best role now is to teach and coach.

Over the years, you built the company from perhaps zero to many millions in sales. Now, the children will be aiming to grow it to twice that much in sales. The skills required to do that will be totally different from the skills you used in the last 30 years. You do need to coach, but you also need to understand that it is a different world. Children need the wisdom and experience of their elders, but the elders need the fresh approach of their children and their ability to see new perspectives. To grow in this age, a business needs tech-savvy minds. Success requires an understanding of fancy software programs, computers, laptops, tablets, and cell phones—in any industry.

If the parents are unwilling to communicate or educate the next generation, the transition becomes much more difficult. I have found that people in their 70s and older don't typically like to talk about their personal finances, their business, or anything to do with money. It's not in their nature to openly talk with their children about income, taxes, gross sales, or their personal net worth. They were not brought up that way. That wall of silence makes the transition harder and longer. It is essential, however, that we break down those barriers and educate the children who will take the company to new heights.

WHO WILL DO WHICH JOB?

If you will be leaving the business to your children, who will do what? If you have only one child, it's easier. That one child needs to understand how to run the business—how to manage a lot of people, how to make the best use of software, which inventory to buy and when, how to manage taxes, and everything it takes to manage a company.

If you have two or three children in the business, you need to divide the workload. They cannot all be the president. One may be good with customers and dealings outside the company, such as going to local chamber of commerce meetings. Another might be good at advertising, inventory, or dealing with vendors and suppliers. Somebody else might be good with the software or with the financials. The family needs to come to an understanding about who is good at what, and then let the children gradually gain control in the areas of their expertise and develop their natural tendencies.

WHO WILL CONTROL
THE COMPANY?

I have worked with a lot of families where two siblings split the voting control of the company evenly, with each having 50 percent. They might get along for a few years, but after a while the more entrepreneurial of the two might want to grow the company, while the other feels that is too risky. Since both have the same voting strength, nothing gets done. They butt heads for several years, and eventually the business starts to fail because the owners are fighting.

Sometimes an even division of stock may be acceptable. I worked with a family in New England where Mom and Dad had sold the business to three sons, who each got a third of the stock. One son was the president; he was an excellent leader and involved in the community. Another was skilled at computer software, inventory, and inside-the-business stuff. The third did a great job at running the warehouse, moving the inventory, and keeping it fresh. The three brothers got along fine, and the arrangement seemed to work perfectly. That's the exception, however.

Since each had a different job, I encouraged them at the beginning to have three different salaries. Whether or not siblings have those positions, the president should be making more than the guy running the warehouse. The three brothers agreed and each had different salaries, but at the end of the year, if the company made a lot of money, they divided the profits into thirds. Sometimes that does work—it depends on family harmony. Usually, however, somebody needs to be the tiebreaker. When I work with families that have multiple children in the business, I normally suggest that somebody have 51 percent voting control.

I have worked with several families in which the parents sell or gift 45 percent to each of two children, so that together they have 90 percent. The parents retain 10 percent. Then, for the next several years, if the kids are fighting about something, Mom and Dad put in their 10 percent worth to settle the matter. That can work well for a while but not so much when the parents get older and are less in tune with the business. In their wills and trusts, they might give their 10 percent to the children equally or give a little more to one of the children so that somebody has 51 percent. In other cases, the parents could gift that final 10 percent after several years, once it's clear that the children are getting along and it's obvious who is taking the lead and should get the voting control.

Sometimes the parents have a daughter working in the business, as well as her husband—or a son and his wife. The parents want to keep both spouses in the company, but in most such cases they don't split the control evenly. The child gets the larger percentage. The child's spouse might get 30 percent or none at all. The parents typically gift or sell the stock to the blood relative—this is how most trust documents are written so that the assets flow from one generation to the next and stay in the bloodline. The sellers want to make sure their net worth stays in the family, in case that daughter-in-law or son-in-law divorces and/or remarries.

I've done transactions many times where a son, daughter, and son-in-law all work in the business, and the children get stock, but the son-in-law does not. Usually, everyone understands that it stays in the family, and they are okay with that. I recently worked with a couple that wanted to sell to their son and a key employee who has been with them for 20 years. They want that key employee, who has done a great job, to get some of the business, but in situations like this, it's never 50/50. Usually, the family member gets 60 or 70 percent, and the key employee buys 30 or 40 percent.

In the overall plan, it is important to consider who will get the stock and who will have the majority voting control. In making such decisions, the business owners need to weigh the importance of keeping the family net worth within the family bloodlines.

INDUSTRY TRAINING

Training and education are very important to help the next generation take your company to the next level. A lot of children and key employees who have been working for a family-held business are obviously proficient in certain areas, such as ordering inventory or advertising, but may not have training or experience in working with taxes for the company, negotiating lines of credit with your banker, or dealing with vendors and distributors. During the next two to three years, you, as the coach, need to start working with your successors on these important areas.

A good friend of mine in Colorado, who died several years ago, had built a very large company, and in the headquarters, his 45-year-old son sat in an office about 60 feet from his. The problem was, his son never got invited to meetings with the bankers, lawyers, accountants, or business associates. At the age of 45, that son—who had worked in the company for at least 15 years and was expected to take over—had never seen a corporate tax return. This is a good example of how not to be a coach.

Training and education—not only in the old ways that got the company to where it is today but also in the newest techniques—and the best-in-class ideas need to be absorbed by your children or key employees who will be taking over the company.

For example, the franchisors and cooperative organizations, to which a lot of small businesses belong, often offer training. They frequently present classes at their annual or biannual conventions with special training in specific areas. In hardware stores, for example, people are trained to run the paint department, learning which product is best for which application, how to mix, how to estimate project requirements, and so on. For jobs in a warehouse, you can get training on handling all the inventory that goes in and out daily.

You can also receive training at local college adult education classes or through online courses. Here in the Midwest, we have an organization called Ivy Tech, an adult training school with many locations. Similar facilities exist in every state.

The next generation needs to learn the latest and best techniques in order to take the company higher in sales and profits. They can learn from their parents, and they can learn from one another. I am often pleased to see at conventions two or three-dozen next-generation people sitting around lunch tables sharing ideas. Many of them are hoping to take over a company. A young man wanting to buy a company in Pennsylvania might be talking with a young woman who just bought a company from her parents in Arizona. Peer-to-peer mentoring is a great way to grow in the business.

BACKWARD ALONG THE TIME LINE

I tell business owners to just give me their time line, whether it's three years or ten years. If you want to sell and retire in, say, five years, we can work backward and figure out just what you should be doing four years from now, three years from now, two, and one. If you give me the number of years, I can give you a plan that we can start fine-tuning.

A lot of business owners seem reluctant to do that. "I don't know when I want to retire. I still want to keep working. I'm not willing to let the kids take over yet." If the kids need more education, then we have five years for them to get it—and for them to prove themselves to their parents. They need to show that they have the enthusiasm and passion for the business. If they don't have what it takes, or if they don't have the interest, then it's time to come up with a different exit plan.

There are two categories of time lines. One is for the stock transition, and the other is for the leadership. The stock might be transferred to the next generation over eight or ten years. The time line for leadership, however, might be only two or three years. For example, the parents may gift or sell 30 or 40 percent of the stock to a son and let him become president in a couple of years. Then, over the next several years, they can gift or sell him the remainder of the stock based on their income needs. By doing that over several years, they can keep the taxes down.

All along the time line, the advisors need to talk to the next generation and explain, "Here's what you've got to do to prove to your Mom and Dad that you know what you're doing. Here's what you need to do next, and here's what we see that's lacking. Here's what you're good at. Here's what you're not good at." Sometimes the outside advisors can see things to which Mom and Dad are blind.

SHIRTSLEEVES TO SHIRTSLEEVES

We need to do this right. Otherwise, within about three generations, the company will be gone, the assets will be gone, and the family's net worth will be gone. "Shirtsleeves to shirtsleeves in three generations" is a phenomenon for business owners all around the world. In Japan and China, they call it "rice paddy to rice paddy in three generations." In Europe, they call it "clogs to clogs in three generations."

Unfortunately, it is true. The first generation is frugal. The farmer saves money, does well, and moves to the city with his family. He launches a business, and it grows. His children live well, but they don't learn from him. They never get their hands dirty, and they learn nothing about business or managing money, so their own children have less to work with, and soon the assets are gone. They eventually have to move back out of town. If they inherit anything, they don't have a clue how to manage it. Within three generations, the company is gone, the assets are gone, and the families have to start all over again. In three generations, shirtsleeves to shirtsleeves. They roll up their sleeves again and start laboring.

I want to help our clients prevent this third generation problem. Your legacy needs to include knowledge. The next generation needs to learn how you did it and respect where the family net worth came from.

CHAPTER SIX

BEYOND THE FAMILY CIRCLE

The father had long hoped that his son would run the company someday. It was a big, successful operation on the West Coast, and the young man indeed was interested in business. His dad brought him aboard and began to groom him.

The son was there for a few years but then left. Three or four years later he returned and tried again, but it just didn't feel right. He wasn't happy. He wanted to run a business but not this one, not with his family in this particular industry. And so he left again.

The father was ready to retire, so he had no choice but to find another buyer within the industry. Since it was a very profitable company, making millions of dollars every year, he was able to sell it for a nice profit. He got a fair price for it, and he had plenty of cash to live on in retirement—but his vision of the business staying in the family just wasn't going to happen.

In the previous chapter, we talked about selling inside the family. Now let's talk about selling outside the family circle—either because there are no children or because they have chosen other careers and don't want the business.

The owner may want to sell to a key manager, if that person is interested. Some key employees with an entrepreneurial spirit are willing to take on a lot of debt to purchase a company. About 15 to 20 percent of the time, key employees become the buyer. Or the company could be sold to someone else within the industry—a strategic purchase, as it's known on Wall Street.

We have been working with a couple whose children decided long ago not to take over the store and they pursued other careers. The couple does have a key manager who is competent to run the business. We have prepared the valuations and figured the cash flows, the financing, and the amortization schedules. The owners will present that package to their key manager, who will be able to see all the financials that he would take to a bank if he were to pursue a loan. The owners will probably have to finance part of it.

In cases such as this, the owners may not find another buyer in the industry. Similar companies are too far away to be interested. The couple's only choice is to sell to that key manager to keep the business going for another 10 or 20 years. The manager would get a pay raise and be able to build equity for himself. The couple has their fingers crossed that he will want to take on some debt and buy the business.

Another client has two stores and is planning to sell to an outside buyer. He, too, has children who don't want the business. The stores make a little bit of money each year, but he hasn't aggressively managed them to make a lot of profit. He does a lot of charitable things for the community, such as sponsoring Little League teams and basketball teams. But now it's time to retire. He's getting tired of getting up at six or seven every morning, seven days a week.

We have encouraged him in the last six months to start demonstrating the potential for greater profitability. He had been paying for all of his employees' health insurance. He couldn't afford it anymore because in early 2014 his premium went up 30 percent, due to the changes in the health insurance industry. He dropped the company health insurance, thereby showing a little more profitability and cash flow.

For 30 years, he hadn't thought much about the company's value. Now that he is about to show the company to somebody else, it is high time that he did so. It's time to make the business look better. We do have a potential buyer, someone in the industry who probably wants to buy those two stores because they're in good cities. We'll get the company sold, but if he had aggressively managed it the last five years, we probably could have gotten more money for it.

SELLING TO KEY MANAGERS

Business owners often feel so comfortable with the competence of their longtime key managers that they can take a two-week vacation without worry. They know the manager does a great job of running the business and protecting it.

Nowadays, the owners can go on vacation and take along a laptop to monitor what's going on back at the store if they have any doubts. They can watch the sales. They can watch inventory. They can watch the cash. They could even tie into the security cameras. That wasn't possible all that long ago.

When the owner feels ready to retire and the key manager has expressed interest in buying the business, we have a valuation done and take a look at the finances so that we can give the manager a pro forma based on the previous three or four years. We put together a due diligence package for the manager to show his accountants and attorneys.

In that proposal, the key manager almost never has a big down payment. Normally it would be a small down payment, but then the manager would start acquiring 10, 20, or 30 percent of the stock over the next four or five years. The seller might give the manager a raise to help make the payments.

While that's happening, the seller, who still controls more than 51 percent of the stock, would continue to get a salary, benefits, and money out of the business as usual. As the key manager gains an increasing share of ownership, he or she will see that this is more than just talk. With such concrete steps, the excitement builds.

While acquiring stock over a three- or four-year period, the manager should meet and work with all the company's accountants, attorneys, bankers, insurance agents, and others. It is important to establish that the manager is really in charge of everything day to day and that the owner is backing away and acting more like the chairman of the board. Not only will the manager be proving his or her mettle, but also the bankers and the others will observe who's running the show.

If the business remains profitable during that time, the manager should be able to go to the bank and qualify for an SBA or other business loan, based on the track record of the last few years. Having already purchased, say, 30 percent over several years, he or she could borrow 60 percent more from the bank, and the owner might accept a personal promissory note for the other 10 percent.

Some owners don't need cash when they give up control. They don't want the manager to go to the bank; instead, they will take back a promissory note for perhaps 70 percent. Then the buyer makes payments to the seller for 10 or 15 years. Every transaction is different, and there are various ways to design a sale between the owner and the key manager.

If the owner is selling to a key employee, the cash flow must work over time. The owner needs to know that, instead of getting a $50,000 check up front, he will continue to get his salary. He will continue to get his benefits. He will continue to pull money out of the company every year for the next three or four years rather than getting a big check up front.

There are ways to make it work. The most important thing is whether this manager can really run the business. I ask you this: If you go to Florida for six months, are you concerned about the company? If you tell me, "No, we're not concerned. The manager does a great job," then I feel reassured. I can rearrange the numbers, like pieces of a puzzle, but I can't rearrange the key manager's ability to handle the business. The manager must be able to handle the finances, the advertising, the hiring and firing, the inventory, and the customers— and instill confidence in all of them. That's the part I can't analyze. I'm not in that store to watch the manager handle every aspect of the business. The owner has to be comfortable that this person can make it work.

TRANSFERRING STOCK TO KEY EMPLOYEES

Sometimes the seller can arrange for some gifting to a key employee. Gifting is more acceptable to the IRS if it's for a son or daughter. The IRS is more strict if you're trying to gift to a key employee, but it does work sometimes.

Some owners consider key employees to be like adopted sons and daughters. They've been there for so long they're part of the family. Sometimes they come to Thanksgiving dinner. Sometimes they go on vacation together or on hunting and fishing trips. In such a close relationship, gifting might be a possibility, although the IRS will treat it somewhat differently than it does for blood relatives.

The owner might wish to transfer 20, 30, even up to 49 percent ownership. Before you give up 51 percent control of a company, you want to make sure that everything is perfect. At the point of decision, we have an important board meeting. We want to know if everything is perfect. Before the owners agree to give up more than half the control, are they confident that this person is competent? If so, then we can finish the transaction.

As long as you have 51 percent ownership, you can control the risk. Once somebody else has 51 percent, then you can no longer control the risk. You're along for the ride. You want to make sure that documents are signed and your retirement security is in place before you get to that point.

Whenever you start selling to a key employee, even at 10 percent, you want to make sure the legal documents are in place. Does the key employee have good wills and trusts? On the same day that the key employee gets the stock certificate, he or she also should be signing the buy-sell agreement. You need it to protect the company—as we see in Chapter 8.

SELLING TO ANOTHER BUSINESS IN YOUR INDUSTRY

If you are selling to someone in your industry other than a key manager, that buyer already knows the industry. People who have been in the business for 30 or 40 years know what the finances should look like. They know how to quickly analyze inventory, equipment, trucks, and warehouses—everything that's needed for the business. They can look at everything quickly and know if they're interested.

Then the main thing is to try and negotiate a fair price. Normally, we can get a little more if we're selling to somebody in the industry. As I pointed out earlier, the buyer already has a back office of people who handle all the finances. If we can reduce the number of employees, that immediately gives the buyer more cash flow. If the owner's EBITDA is $200,000, it quickly could go to $300,000 if the buyer reduces the payroll, making the company more valuable to the buyer.

Also, computers and software are expensive. It's easy for a company to spend $20,000 or $30,000 a year on the technology to manage the sales and the inventory. If the buyer already has all of that software, they don't need to buy your software. If you're spending $20,000 or

$30,000 a year, the buyer won't renew the contract. That gives them that much more in profit.

In short, when you're selling a company, consider the buyer's perspective. What is the buyer getting, keeping, or not going to need? Maybe the buyer already has ten delivery trucks. If you have five and he only needs two, he can get rid of three delivery trucks. That greatly reduces the maintenance cost that you have been paying.

HELP FOR THE NEGOTIATIONS

I usually suggest to sellers that they not negotiate the sale. They normally don't get the best price. They have trouble seeing things objectively. You want somebody to represent you who is more independent and realistic. That's why many people have asked our firm to help them sell their businesses and talk to the buyer.

In the real estate industry, you hire an agent to sell your house. When potential buyers want to see your house, the agent suggests that you leave the premises during the showing. That's because real estate agents know from experience that the owners aren't necessarily the best people to advance the deal.

Of the 32 million closely held businesses in the United States, very few have sales of $50 million to $100 million or more, and those companies can hire a Wall Street expert to help them. But most businesses are far smaller. Many have only a few million in sales. It's a great way to support a family, but you're probably not going to be able to hire a merger and acquisition company from Wall Street to help you sell the business.

There are business brokers in this country who help a lot of small businesses, but be careful if you hire one of them. Make sure the broker has a great track record in your industry. There are some good ones, but there also are some that don't know anything about your industry and don't have any potential buyers.

This is where a co-op manager or franchisor could be a match-maker or go-between. The co-op or franchisor might know, for example, that in Iowa there are three or four companies that want to grow and would be interested in buying, so when somebody in Iowa wants to sell, they can immediately put them in touch. The larger franchisors and co-ops accumulate knowledge in each state about the logical buyers and sellers.

WHEN EVERYONE WINS

As we have seen, there are a lot of options in selling, and the seller can negotiate a lot of advantages besides a higher price. There are many ways to sell, and there are many ways to be paid besides just getting one big fat check. The owner could collect $40,000 to $60,000 a year as a consultant to help with the transition, intro-ducing the buyer to members of the community and to customers and assisting with employee relations. I also have mentioned other sources of income for the seller: non-compete contracts and deferred compensation. Much depends on who the buyer is.

A good buyer and a good seller, even when unrelated, can negotiate to figure out the best way to help both of them. It's a good deal when they both get advantages and negotiate overall benefits for both buyer and seller. Those are what I call the fun projects, where everybody wins.

EMPLOYEE STOCK OWNERSHIP PLANS (ESOPs)

For some companies, the buyer outside the family circle might come in the form of an Employee Stock Ownership Plan or ESOP.

The ESOP is a qualified employee benefit plan that is similar to profit sharing. It is run by trustees, usually the owner and four or five employees. The trustees can go to a bank and borrow the amount needed to buy the company. If the bank is comfortable that the company is profitable and approves the loan, the ESOP uses that money to buy the stock from the retiring owner. The seller gets his or her money, along with potential tax benefits.

The ESOP then owns 100 percent of the company. The company makes annual contributions to the ESOP, which uses that cash flow to pay off the bank loan. The company is allowed to contribute up to 25 percent of payroll to the plan. If the payroll is a million dollars a year, for example, the contribution can be $250,000—and it is a tax deduction for the company.

For this option, the business normally would need at least 40 or 50 employees, preferably more. It's harder to make it work if there are fewer employees, because the ESOP's cash flow is based on the total payroll. In a small workforce, 25 percent of the payroll might only be $60,000 or $80,000 a year. That won't pay off much of a bank loan. The purchase price would have to be very low, plus the annual maintenance costs are at least $25,000 to $30,000. In addition, if an ESOP is to work well, the business must have great managers. With key personnel walking away, does the workforce still have two or three people who can run the company for the next 20 years?

An ESOP is a possibility, but it's not perfect for everybody. At our firm, we might do one a year. We have special attorneys who do the documents, and special valuation companies to make sure that the ESOP has enough cash flow to afford a bank loan.

Setting this up calls for a lot of expertise. You're preparing a qualified pension plan. The legal fees might be $20,000 or $30,000. The valuation fees might be $20,000 or $25,000. It might be $40,000 or $50,000 the first year, and then it might be $20,000 or $30,000 every year to manage all of the legal documents. It's not a cheap transaction, but it is beneficial if it works perfectly for everybody. The owner can save taxes, and the employees wind up owning 100 percent of the company. If they can make that company grow at 10 or 15 percent a year for a decade or more, the employees will have very good retirement accounts.

It works like this: Inside the ESOP trust, every employee has a small percentage of ownership, based on their age and pay. The higher paid people might get 3 or 4 percent. The lower paid people might get 1 or 2 percent. Everybody in the company owns a piece of it. All of the stock is held inside the trust, just like a pension. It's controlled by the trustees.

I like ESOPs. I like the idea of employees owning a piece of the company where they work every day. But there are pros and cons to everything. It has to be the right kind of company, the workforce needs to have the management talent to run it, and there has to be a sufficient number of employees to pull it off. Before you go down that path, do plenty of research.

CHAPTER SEVEN

WHAT IS YOUR BUSINESS WORTH?

B usiness owners often think their company is worth more than it really is. But after we peel back the layers and analyze the financial statements and tax returns, they begin to see the difference between wishful thinking and reality.

We do a lot of valuations, and quite often, after we go through all the numbers, the owners concede that they were overestimating. It's similar to homeowners awakening to the true value of their house after a real estate agent shows them recent sales prices of comparable properties. It's a reality check, and sometimes you need someone else's perspective.

Not all valuations will be spot-on, of course, and that's one reason I started a valuation company 20 years ago. When I needed an appraisal for a heating and air conditioning company, a lumberyard, or a carpet store, the bank would choose somebody who had never worked with that industry. The results were quite often too high or too low. They were not using the right formulas.

Today, we do valuations for the six or seven industries in which we specialize. We know everything about them, and we have helped hundreds of business owners sell their companies. We have been gratified to see how well the ultimate sales price matches up with our valuation. When we are not so familiar with an industry, however, we look for an appraiser with specific experience in it.

Some business owners get more than one valuation. The seller will get one, and sometimes the buyer will get another for a second opinion. Then they share the results and negotiate. Quite often, valuations are done because a business partner is selling his portion of the company to the other partner. Under terms of the buy-sell agreement, each party has a valuation done, and if necessary the two appraisers get somebody to do a third valuation and they average the three figures.

METHODS OF VALUATION

Generally, any valuation company will analyze the company's tax returns, balance sheets, and profit and loss statements. There are eight or ten methods of valuing a business, but they all involve two primary ideas. For most companies, the buyer will be looking at the real assets after adjustments and at the real cash flow.

The net asset approach looks at all of the assets and liabilities of a company. The capitalization rate approach looks at the owner's usable cash flow. There are variations, but those are the two primary methods. It all boils down to either assets or cash flow or both.

Another consideration is the type of business entity, whether it's a C corporation, an S corporation, an LLC, or a partnership. People who own C corporations normally have a lower cost basis in their stock value. People who have an S corporation or LLC may have a higher basis in the company.

Valuations are a little different for each industry. If you created a software company, for example, the valuation is based on the cash flow of that software company. You probably wouldn't have big factories and delivery trucks. You just have software.

However, for most of the millions of US business owners, the appraiser will look at assets and adjust them up and down to be realistic, and they will also look at the real cash flow. The tax return might show $100,000 of profit, but the usable cash flow is actually higher.

A common adjustment that we would make to a typical financial statement would be to the inventory. Sometimes the financial statement will say the business has $600,000 of inventory, but in reality it's closer to $800,000. We need to add $200,000. Sometimes companies have $600,000 of inventory, but that includes $50,000 of items that have been on the shelves for three or four years. Those items are considered obsolete. For a realistic valuation, we would adjust the figure on the financial statement to $550,000.

Sometimes we adjust accounts receivable. If you have $50,000 of accounts receivable, you may have $5,000 that you're not going to be able to collect because two or three customers filed bankruptcy. There are all kinds of reasons that you don't collect all of your accounts receivable. We make those adjustments.

After all the necessary adjustments, we come up with a realistic value. If I am looking at a company with a million dollars in stockholders' equity, the adjustments might bring that up to $1.3 million or down to $900,000.

The other major consideration is the usable cash flow (also known as EBITDA, as I explain in Chapter 2). The higher the cash flow, the more valuable your business will be. In order to come up with the adjusted usable cash flow, we would add back some of the expensed items. If the owner takes out a high salary, we might add back some of his salary to bring it back to the industry average. We add back the depreciation. We add back interest. If the owner takes customers or vendors out to the country club and buys them lunch, we add back the country club dues. We would add back some of the travel expenses. And afterward, the $100,000 in profit, as listed on the tax return, becomes more like $200,000—a far more attractive cash flow for a buyer.

TIME TO GET REAL

So many factors must be taken into consideration in the overall valuation of a business—including its location and its inventory, as I point out in Chapter 3. "Location, location, location" is an adage in the real estate profession. Are you at a great location, on a major intersection, perhaps in the newest shopping center? Or are you in an old building on a rundown street?

Many owners ran the business for 30 or 40 years without paying much attention to how the tax returns or financial statements look.

They haven't thought much about how the location—or the quality and quantity of the inventory—would eventually affect the value of their business. They haven't turned their attention to making the company operations look great during the last five years before the sale.

As a result, when it's time to sell the business, it doesn't have its best face on. That's why we have to clean everything up and make it look realistic. We look at every item, every number. Is it all accurate? What is the real inventory? Just how profitable has the business really been? You may have more to offer than you thought. This is the time to tell potential buyers all the good details that perhaps you haven't been keeping track of over the years.

A lot goes into valuations, and this is where the rubber meets the road. A good valuation report is typically a starting point for most owners. What is the business really worth? Then, what would you have left after taxes if you sell it? Is that enough to live on the rest of your life? In short, are you able to retire or move on to the next chapter of your life?

CHAPTER EIGHT

NORMAL DOCUMENTS
NEEDED

"All I need is a will," people tell me at conferences. "I've just got a simple little business, and my wife and I run it." Let me assure you, if you run a business, you will need more than that. Legal documents are essential for protecting the business owner, the spouse, the children, and the company.

Most business owners need to consider the documents that we talk about in this chapter, and those with a high net worth—of more than $8 or $10 million—will probably need more details in their documents and more complicated planning techniques. Here we discuss the documents that 90 percent of all business owners should have.

Banks require signatures and vendors require signatures. A lot of business activities require the controlling stockholder's signature, so that's why being prepared for the business owner's death or disability is very important.

We normally work on three or four estates of business owners every year, helping the family and attorneys. When I speak on estate planning, I ask the audience: "What do you suppose is the most difficult thing we deal with in the first few weeks after the business owner dies?" Seldom does anyone guess that the answer is "passwords."

When the owner dies and we don't know the passwords, how do we transfer cash into the checking account to cover payroll? How do we get access to the company's financial data? A decade or two ago, you had maybe one password. Now you might have ten. Almost anyone who has ever forgotten a password has had to jump through hoops to get a new one. When the account owner dies, it can be even harder.

A few years ago, a business owner in Montana hit a tree while skiing and died. It was on a Wednesday, and payday was on Friday. The wife and managers had no cash to cover payroll, because the money needed to be transferred from a different account. On Friday morning, two friends who owned businesses lent money to the company in order to cover payroll.

A lot of business owners don't think about such contingencies. If you get ill or die, the show must go on. There won't always be friends willing to help in a pinch like that. If you had a heart attack or serious car accident a month from now, who would be able to run the business for the next 60 to 90 days? Would someone be able to transfer cash? Would there be enough cash to cover payroll? Who would renew the line of credit with the bank to buy inventory? You need answers to all of these questions, and you need to get them written down.

Segregate the duties. Have one person handle the cash and the deposits and another order inventory. That puts checks and balances into place while you're at the hospital recuperating. Who will be doing what? Who has the right to hire and fire employees? Who can change the work schedule? Who's going to open up the office tomorrow morning, and who's going to close it? Who orders inventory each week? We need to get all of that in writing, divide up the workload, and define responsibilities. It's also a good idea to let your attorney, accountant, and banker know who your handpicked people are.

I usually talk with people about seven basic documents. Yes, you need far more than just a will—but that's a good place to begin.

YOUR LAST WILL AND TESTAMENT

In a will, you typically leave personal items to specific people. The will is written to instruct others on what you would do if you were still alive. Perhaps you want some assets to go to a trust, other assets to go to your spouse, and others to a son or daughter.

There are a lot of things that you can put in a will. Besides the personal items, you could leave money to your favorite charities. Most people would leave assets to charities in a trust document, but you could do it in your will.

Business owners often have what are called pour-over wills. The will basically pours over the important assets into a trust, and the trust acts like a basket to hold and manage those assets for the family, business, and heirs. Normally you would leave all of your important assets—life insurance, the stock in your company, real estate—to a trust.

You should pull out your will and review it at least every five years. If your will is five years old, it's too old. If it's more than ten years old, it's way too old. Tax laws have been changing almost every year, and your net worth and family situation have probably changed as well.

Every young family needs a will, even if it's a son or daughter who does not yet have stock in the family business. Even if they have zero net worth, I usually tell young people that they still need a will for one basic reason: it's where you can name the guardian of your child. If something happens to you and you don't have a will, some judge will make that decision for you.

REVOCABLE LIVING TRUST

A trust is a manager of assets. A will doesn't manage assets, but it can pour over into a trust, which is probably the most important document for you personally. Some people argue that not everybody needs a trust, which is probably true. If your net worth is very low, you probably don't need a trust. But if you have assets to protect and your net worth is more than $1,000,000 and growing, then you probably need a trust to manage and protect those assets.

You arrange to put everything into that one basket, and then you appoint a trustee, who might be your spouse. You also name a successor trustee—perhaps one of your children or your brother. It could also be a bank trust department, although most people would rather pick a family member and then hire experts to help them.

While you are alive, you can change a revocable living trust anytime. You can change a paragraph. You can change names. You can change anything you want. Upon death, the trust becomes irrevocable. The language in the trust will stay that way, and everything will happen as you have instructed.

Typically, lawyers break the trust into two pieces. Trust A might be the marital trust, and Trust B might be the family trust, which is sometimes called the credit trust. The credit trust would receive the amount of money equal to the federal estate tax exemption. In 2015 the exemption would be $5,430,000. For example, if a married couple had a net worth of $6.4 million, $5.4 million would go into the credit trust and the remaining $1 million would go into the marital trust. This is done so that your estate would qualify for the largest estate tax savings.

When I started in business back in 1970, the federal estate tax exemption was around $60,000; later in that same decade, it jumped to $175,000. If your net worth was less than that amount, you would not pay any federal estate tax. A few years later, the exemption jumped to $600,000. It was $1 million for two or three years, then in 2010 there was no federal estate tax. A few years ago, Congress passed a law that made the exemption $5.1 million, and that has bumped up with inflation. For 2015, it's $5.43 million. If you're married, it's double that—so if your combined net worth is less than $10.86 million, you won't pay federal estate tax.

However, you still must pay any estate or inheritance tax that your state requires, and in some states, that's pretty high. Some still have a $1 million exemption; if your combined net worth is $9 million, you would pay no federal tax but would pay state taxes on $8 million. In addition, you would still have attorney's fees to pay for probate. The probate expense might be minimized by having a trust, but there would still be work for the attorneys to handle.

Upon death, the revocable living trust can be broken into the two pieces mentioned above—the family or credit trust and the marital trust. Here's an example of how that works: Most documents would direct that the family or credit trust contain the amount of the estate up to the federal exemption in order to qualify for that exemption. Anything above that would go to the marital trust. Let's say you have a $5 million estate and that you set up your trust several years ago, when the exemption was only $2 million. At that time, you thought you would be putting $2 million into the family trust and $3 million into the marital trust. However, now that the exemption is much higher, would you want the entire estate to go into the family trust and nothing into the marital trust? Because the law changed, zero dollars would go to the spouse's marital trust. This may change your overall distribution to children, grandchildren, and charities and also could be a problem for a second or third marriage.

The change in exemption calls for a change in estate planning. A business owner needs to take these matters into consideration when deciding whether the company stock should go into the marital trust or the family trust. Who will be the trustee? Who will have voting control for the stock? Who will run the company? That's why it is important to review these documents regularly.

Trusts are designed a little differently in community property states, like California, Arizona, and Nevada. Each spouse would have a will, and then there would be one trust for the two of them. But in common law states like Indiana, Pennsylvania, and Florida, each spouse would have individual documents. The husband would have a will and a trust, and the wife would have a will and a trust.

The trust document could say, basically: "Manage the assets for my spouse. Give her all of the income. Give her principal if she needs it. Upon her death, I want this much to go to charity and this much to my children when they turn 30 or 40 or 50. If my children are not alive and if they have children, I want their share to go to the grandchildren when they turn 21." The document passes assets down the family tree so that they stay in the family. The trust, in essence, manages the assets for the family's benefit. The document can easily be 20 to 40 pages long. If the trust is four pages, there's a problem: You can't say everything necessary in four pages.

If you transferred 100 percent of the company stock to your trust, the trustees will vote those shares. If you own real estate in an LLC and transferred the ownership to your trust, the trustees will vote those shares and manage those assets. The trust document controls exactly which road the assets go down.

GENERAL DURABLE POWER FOR FINANCIAL CARE

Upon your death, the will and the trust will dictate what happens. If you're alive but incapacitated—for example, you're in a coma or have advanced Alzheimer's—the durable powers are in charge. A good estate tax attorney normally will prepare five documents at the same time—the will, the trust, the two durable powers, and a living will, which is an advance directive on medical care if you can no longer speak for yourself.

Under the durable power for financial care, you could appoint your spouse or one of your children, for example, to sign checks and to pay monthly expenses if you were disabled. They would have the power to sell some stocks in your investment account and put that cash in your checking account.

Besides paying normal bills each month, that person also should have authorization to continue any gifting program that is part of the overall business and personal asset protection plan. Some durable powers give the designated person the power to continue making gifts, and some do not. If you're gifting stock to children, you want to make sure that the gifting power is in that document. Some states have it built in, but in some states the lawyers have to add it.

DURABLE POWER OF ATTORNEY FOR HEALTH CARE

If you should become incapacitated, somebody has to be authorized to talk to the medical personnel. You might think your spouse should be empowered to talk to anybody. But with federal HIPAA laws, even spouses need a legal document authorizing each other to make medical decisions.

That's why you need a separate durable power for health care. You appoint your spouse, daughter, son, or whomever to have the power to talk to the doctors. If you have a specific doctor or hospital in mind, make sure that each has a copy of the durable power for health care in their file now.

BUY-SELL OR STOCK REDEMPTION AGREEMENT

If there are two or more stockholders in a company, the buy-sell agreement is a crucial document. It is sometimes called a stock redemption agreement, a shareholder agreement, or a cross-purchase agreement. This is a separate legal document that spells out what happens to the stock in case of certain "trigger points": death, divorce, disability, personal bankruptcy, termination, retirement, or the sale of stock.

Let's say two friends started a company 30 years ago. It has become a big company, and they need to have in place a stock redemption agreement covering those trigger points. Stock redemption agreements always cover death. If one partner dies, the agreement says the other has the right to buy him or her out. The agreement should contain a formula for valuing the stock in the company.

Sometimes the agreements mention life insurance, and an insurance agent sells each partner a policy. Let's say two partners bought half a million dollars of life insurance on each other. But that was 15 years ago, and now the company is worth $2 million each, totaling $4 million—and they only have half a million of insurance on each other. If one partner were to die, the other would use the $500,000 as a partial down payment. The agreement needs to say that the remaining partner has the ability to sign a promissory note for $1.5 million and pay over time. If it doesn't, the partner might be forced to quickly go to a bank and try to borrow the money.

The payments over time must be spelled out in the agreement. A lot of buy-sell agreements don't have that language. They don't specify, in effect, "You have ten years to pay my family." That can create a lot of heartache between partners and families when someone dies.

The agreement should state that in case of divorce, the stock cannot leave the family. The majority stockholders don't want an ex-spouse owning a piece of the business, so the language needs to prohibit giving away stock as part of a divorce settlement.

Disability is another major consideration. The agreement often doesn't cover it properly. A lot of documents more or less say, "If I'm permanently disabled, somebody can buy my stock." But how do you define "permanent"? Is five years permanent? Fifteen years? How do you define "disability"? If I can still sit up in bed, am I disabled? If I can come to the office for an hour if someone brings me, am I disabled? Typically, it comes down to this: If you don't show up to work for 12 months to fulfill your job description, then you're disabled and the company or other stockholders can buy you out. Some cut it off at six months. Disability should relate to job performance or function, but that's not worded well in most buy-sell agreements.

Another trigger is personal bankruptcy. If a stockholder—the owner's son, for example—has a lot of credit cards and has to file for personal bankruptcy, he cannot give his stock in the business to somebody else. Another is termination: If the owner fires his daughter for stealing money or for doing a bad job, she has to sell her stock back to the company. And retirement: If one partner retires, the other has a right to buy that portion of the business over a specific number of years, as determined in the agreement.

In working with hundreds of families, the two triggers I see most commonly are divorce and disability. Business owners die, but more often they become disabled or get divorced. The wording in this agreement must be precise, because the buy-sell document will control the stock.

In a corporation, like an S corporation or a C corporation, we would have a separate buy-sell document signed by all stockholders. A corporation has bylaws and minutes, and the buy-sell agreement usually is discussed in the minutes and attached. For LLCs, it is a little different. For most LLCs, attorneys will prepare what is called an operating agreement. An operating agreement usually has a section that talks about stock transfers, and that's where the lawyer can put the language about all those trigger points.

BUSINESS LETTER

I usually suggest that the owners prepare what is known as a business letter, in which they spell out who would run the business if they were unable to do so. The letter would include the owner's passwords and other important information for the company.

That letter would go into a safe, and the business owner would make sure that someone trustworthy would be able to gain access to it. If something were to happen to the business owner, the entrusted person could quickly obtain that business letter. Everyone would know the function that you intended for them, rather than guessing or arguing about it.

The business letter should indicate who would sign checks for the company, who would order inventory, and who would take care of payroll. Also you should indicate who would be responsible for hiring and firing employees, handling the advertising, and all other major aspects of running your business. Hopefully, your business letter will not only let all of your employees know who is in charge, but also encourage them to work together and do what is right for the business.

PERSONAL LETTER

Let's say a company has children working in the business and a ten-year succession plan, but the owner dies in the third year. In such a case, it's good to have a personal letter outlining the direction that the successors should take.

It would say, more or less, "We have been working on our business succession plan, and if something happens to me, I want my daughter Suzanne and my son Robert to work cooperatively to accomplish the following"—and then the letter would outline how the family would work together to continue the business. Also, instructions would be included in your will or trust.

Most family businesses don't have a letter like that, so if Mom and Dad were to die in a car accident, the kids could end up fighting about who's going to be president. Who's going to be in control? Who's going to do what? Even if there is a letter, there might be some squabbling, but the letter can go a long way toward smoothing out conflicts. The children can see that their parents thought these things through and that they cared enough to take the time to directly state their wishes in writing.

The documents that I have discussed here are a good starting point. Make sure you find great attorneys, accountants and financial advisors who will suggest new documents and important changes to consider when the time is right. Update the documents every four or five years, because people and situations change.

Sometimes a couple will have an attorney prepare wills and trusts with all the right language and then go home happy with themselves. They put those documents in a safe and congratulate themselves for doing the right thing. But their home is in joint name. Their checking accounts are in joint name. All of their assets are in joint name. The beneficiaries of the life insurance policies are each other. If you own property in joint name, when you die it goes to your spouse. It doesn't go to your trust. The trust could wind up with nothing in it.

Normally we would leave the house in joint name, because we want the surviving spouse to get the house outright. But stock in the corporation should probably go into the trust. If you have an LLC, the shares, or "units," of the LLC would go into your trust. Then your spouse or child or somebody will be the manager of that trust, with the help of your team of advisors.

If you don't follow through, it's like having a blueprint where the lines don't touch. You can't build a house where the walls don't come together. You need to create the wills and trusts and fund the trusts by changing the ownership of some assets and changing the beneficiaries where necessary. If you have a large IRA, it's payable to your spouse, but what if both of you die together in an accident? The language can send that money into the trust to be managed on behalf of your children.

You have to think through what will happen and where the assets will be going. How will your net worth be protected for your children and your grandchildren? A good estate tax attorney can help you with that sort of decision making. You need a specialist.

CHAPTER NINE

MANAGING YOUR NET WORTH

I have a client out West who transitioned the ownership of his company to a son, who is doing a wonderful job. The father has severe diabetes and uses a wheelchair. He has a wife and other children, but he has put the business in the hands of the one son.

This calls for careful management of all his other assets as well: stocks, bonds, real estate, and everything else he has. We have to make sure that the family is protected and the investments are allocated for the correct ownership. His trust documents and beneficiaries need to be set up properly.

We have finished his business plan to transition the company, but that was only half the job. Now comes the task of wealth management for the future. We need to give this gentleman, whose diabetes worsens by the year, a financial plan that will see to his needs and those of his family.

In the first eight chapters we've talked about a lot of financial topics that affect business owners and their succession planning. Now, if you've done all the other items properly, it's time to think about yourself and your future.

A lot of business owners are going to live a long time in retirement. In the United States right now there are 53,000 people who are age 100 or older. Insurance actuaries tell us that somebody who is age 70 has a 50 percent chance of living to 93. For a married couple, if both spouses are 65, there's a 25 percent chance that one of them will live to be 97.

So if you're 65 years old, there's a good chance that you're going to need assets that will produce an income for 20 or 30 more years. You spent 30 years growing the company, you sold it yesterday, and now whatever your net worth is will have to take care of you for the next 25 years. You have to give a lot of thought to how you will conservatively manage these assets. Not too many decades ago, when Social Security was founded, someone who retired at 65 was usually dead by age 70. But with modern medicine and better health habits, people are living into their 90s and beyond. Your money must last a long time.

A NEW SET OF SKILLS

Let's talk about managing your net worth for you, your family, and all of your beneficiaries. You want to develop a plan so that these assets can be properly channeled through ownership and beneficiaries for three or four generations. There is about a 30 percent chance that your grandchild who was born recently will live to be 100. So if you want to manage assets for your grandkids, you really need a 100-year plan, not a 20-year plan.

A lot of people don't think about that, and maybe some don't care. But as their net worth gets higher, perhaps $1 million or $5 million, they often want to pass it on to their children and maybe something to their grandchildren. And those with a net worth of $20 million or $50 million want it to last many generations.

The facts of the matter are clear: In managing net worth, most people want to develop a plan to reduce risk, minimize expenses, and make the family net worth last a long time. Someone who has run a factory knows how to manufacture the product. Someone who has run a store knows how to sell inventory. They know how to manage employees. But now those days are over. They are left with some cash and perhaps some real estate. This calls for a different kind of management. Do they know how to handle those assets? Some do, but many do not—they lack that particular skill.

A few years ago a couple came into my office with a sad story. They had sold their business for $3 million and invested all of it in the stock market. That was around 2008. Then in 2009 when the recession hit, their $3 million quickly dwindled to $2 million. They immediately sold out of the market, and they were scared to death because they had invested all of their money in stocks. Some of them were good blue-chip stocks, but everything dropped when the tide went out. They had worked for many years to build up their company and get that $3 million, but they did not manage or minimize the risk on their hard-earned sales proceeds.

I don't want other people to make that mistake. Managing assets is completely different than managing a business. It is imperative that you start developing those skills or find the people who can do it for you. You need an independent, fee-only registered investment advisor. I explain that further in Chapter 10.

THE BEQUEST OF KNOWLEDGE

If your net worth was $10 million when you sold the company, we might suggest that you put $3 million or $4 million into a limited liability company (LLC). Let's say John and Mary Smith are the owners of a company. We might put $7 million into trust accounts for their future and $3 million into an LLC. That $3 million can be managed for the owners inside that limited liability company.

The reason we would suggest this is to start moving some ownership percentage to the children. John and Mary have three children, so we figure out what the shares are worth in the LLC and then start gifting 10 to 20 percent to each child. On day one, Mom and Dad own 100 percent of the LLC. But after four or five years, they may own only 10 percent. Ninety percent has been gifted to the three children.

Over the next 20 years, as that LLC and those investments grow in value, 90 percent of that growth is going to be in the children's estate, and only 10 percent would be in Mom and Dad's estate when they die. Not only is that a way to reduce estate tax, but more importantly the process and the annual meetings teach the children how to manage assets. It can be risky for a young person who has been making maybe $60,000 a year at some job to suddenly inherit $1 million. How is he or she to know what to do? Nobody has ever spent one minute talking to the young person about allocations and diversification. What's a municipal bond? What's a blue chip? What's a dividend? They often don't understand the basics.

Those heirs would be much better off if we could all sit down regularly at the kitchen table over the course of the next ten years and talk about money. "Here's how we're allocating this. We've got this amount in bonds. We've got this amount in stocks, and they're paying dividends, and we've got this in real estate and this much in oil and gas. Here's how we're reducing expenses and commissions. And here's why municipal bonds make sense in your tax bracket."

"What's a municipal bond?" the children will surely ask. You can tell them. And you can expect that they will ask: "What's tax-free income?" Don't be surprised. Nobody knows until they are taught.

We can spend the next several years using the LLC as a teaching tool so that the whole family can talk about asset management. It's a way to train the kids so that they have a higher level of financial sophistication when Mom and Dad die. That's the way to get your assets to endure for generations.

The other choice is to do nothing. Let the kids inherit the money. They'll blow through it, and then your grandkids will get nothing. Unless the children learn good basic financial management, the grandkids are unlikely to inherit much money. They are more likely to inherit an old rusty sports car.

You are bequeathing more than just money, more than just your business. You are bequeathing knowledge—whether about running a company or about handling assets in good times and bad.

You have spent decades learning what works and doesn't work. An immensely valuable asset to pass on to the next generation is the wisdom gained from that trial and error and growth. If you can pass on that knowledge, you will protect your loved ones and you will protect the family's net worth.

THE "FAMILY CLASSROOM"

Over the years, I have found several different ways to help transfer financial knowledge from the older generation to the younger generation. I call these techniques the "family classroom."

Here are some examples. If the children buy the company, then perhaps you and your spouse could create a board of directors for the company and have quarterly board meetings. Spend a lot of time putting together an agenda for each board meeting, and use those as the teaching classroom to cover important financial topics that will help the children.

If you and your spouse have a net worth of $4 million or more, it might make sense to set up a family investment company. You could set up a simple limited liability company and transfer $1 to $2 million into that LLC. Both you and your spouse and all of your children could be on its board of directors. By having regular meetings with your independent financial advisor, you can discuss every aspect of asset management: reducing expenses, minimizing or eliminating commissions, asset diversification, and review of asset classes. When is the right time to purchase municipal bonds? What's the right percentage of equities and bonds? What types of assets would be appropriate for this investment company in this economic climate? By having regular meetings over a period of years, all of your children and possibly your grandchildren will learn important aspects of managing different types of investments. This knowledge will become invaluable when they inherit a large amount from your personal wills and trusts.

Another type of vehicle that we often use is a private family foundation. Some families that are committed to gifting assets to charity every year like the idea of creating their own foundation that can manage a portion of their net worth for several generations. You've heard of the Ford Foundation and the Rockefeller Foundation. There are thousands of other foundations managed by families who provide a lot of benefits to their communities. Yes, there are tax advantages for creating a private foundation, but the good that you can do for your community far exceeds the tax benefits.

You and your spouse and children can be on the board of directors of the family foundation. Once again, by having regular meetings to make investment management decisions for the foundation, you can teach your children the best ideas for asset management. You will also get your children involved in making charitable decisions as they help run the foundation for many years.

These are just some of the vehicles that you can use not only to help your community and protect your net worth, but also to educate your children and grandchildren on prudent asset management techniques. Receiving a lot of money without financial savvy can be dangerous. Just ask any lottery winner.

PROVISIONS AND INCENTIVES

If for some reason you lack confidence that a child will ever be able to handle the money competently, there are ways to control what the heirs do with it. If somebody has three children and one of them has Down's syndrome or a learning disability, Mom and Dad might want to say in the trust document that they want this child's money to remain in trust for the rest of his or her life, even though the other children's assets will be paid out at age 40 or 50. Some parents, likewise, will decree that an alcoholic or otherwise addicted child's assets remain in trust.

The trust document will state that the money will take care of the children's health, welfare, and support, but there are ways to put language into trusts that build incentives and impose restrictions. When certain milestones are reached—for example, enrollment in college—then a certain amount of money will be distributed. However, the trust might limit tuition payments to six years so that the child doesn't become a professional student. If a child is going to inherit $5 million, we could advance a few hundred thousand dollars just to see how well they handle the money. The trust might say that the child can get a down payment to buy a house. It might set them up in a professional office if they become a doctor or a lawyer and help to pay for the equipment to get the practice going. The language of the trust can govern a wide variety of such situations.

INTO A PROSPEROUS FUTURE

The fundamental question is this: Now that you have sold the company and converted your illiquid business into liquid assets, how do you manage this pile of cash? You will need a lot of documents for protection, and you will have a variety of options, depending on the extent of your net worth.

For some families that are very charitably inclined, we could set up a private family foundation (PFF). For John and Mary Smith, we might set up an LLC or a family partnership to manage some of their liquid assets and get the kids involved to start learning how to manage that amount of money. The kids manage the LLC to provide income for themselves and manage the foundation to provide income for the charities that their parents want to benefit.

There are a lot of tools that we can use as a client's net worth increases. Above all, the children need to understand and appreciate how those assets were accumulated, and they need to learn how to manage those assets for the future. A lot of families don't provide that education, and it is crucial if your net worth is to stay in the family for years to come.

We must plan diligently to avoid the trap of "shirtsleeves to shirtsleeves in three generations." The proceeds of Grandma and Grandpa's hard work and dedication must not be blown before it can benefit the grandchildren. My hope is that this book will help to break that pattern so that a family's net worth will improve the lives of the great grandchildren and well beyond.

CHAPTER TEN

YOUR DREAM TEAM

You probably remember that the US basketball players in the Olympics years ago were called the Dream Team. They were the best of the best. This chapter is about developing a dream team to help you with business decisions, particularly as you anticipate selling your company and moving on to new adventures.

As it should be clear from prior chapters, business owners need to tap into a variety of expertise—a team of several people—to put together a successful business succession plan. You need these people in order to make the process all come together and to maximize profit on the sale. The techniques suggested by your dream team will depend on whether you are selling to a family member, key employee, or someone else in the industry.

Business owners know how to run a company and what their employees need to be doing. But when it comes time to sell a company, there are a lot more legal decisions, tax laws, and business evaluations to think about. Let's take a look at the different types of advisors whom you may want to have on your team.

CORPORATE OR BUSINESS ATTORNEY

Depending on the complexity of your business sale, you may want a corporate or business attorney on your team. If you sell to your family members or key employees, the length of the legal documents will probably be shorter. If you sell to another company in your industry, the length of the documents gets longer and more complex. This is where you need a corporate attorney who is familiar with letters of intent, term sheets, sales documents, and other legal documents that are necessary to sell a business. Perhaps the attorney with whom you have worked for the last 20 or 30 years might be the right choice, or perhaps he or she will want to team up with a special- ist for this one project.

ESTATE TAX ATTORNEY

When you sell your company, the makeup of your assets totally changes. You have sold your first or second largest asset. This is usually a good time to review your wills, revocable living trusts, durable powers, beneficiaries of retirement accounts and life insurance policies, and the titling of all assets that you own.

If your wills and trusts were done five or ten years ago, that's another reason to completely review all of these documents. Your net worth is probably higher, and federal and estate tax laws have changed. Adding an estate tax attorney to your dream team might be a good idea.

Sometimes when our firm is working with business owners, we work with their attorneys and suggest changes to their trust documents in order to distribute assets differently. For example, if a family has three children and the parents just sold the business to one child, we sometimes suggest to their attorney to change the trust documents so that the other two children might receive a larger percentage from the trust and the one child who now owns the business might receive a smaller percentage of the inheritance. Also at this time, it might be appropriate to change the beneficiaries of some of the assets, such as individual retirement accounts or life insurance policies.

This is usually a perfect time to reassess all of the assets in your net worth and make sure that everything is titled properly and that all of the documents are updated to help protect your net worth.

ACCOUNTANT

Your accountants are very important members of your dream team who have helped you prepare your corporate and personal tax returns for many years. They will help you calculate your cost basis for the sale of the company and estimate any long-term capital gains tax, ordinary income tax, recapture, or any other federal or state taxes that need to be paid.

You may have one accountant who can help with corporate decisions for saving income taxes on the sale, and you may have a separate accountant reviewing your personal tax returns and making suggestions for saving taxes and structuring the sale to benefit you personally.

If you're selling to one of your children or key employees, the accountants should look at their income tax bracket and help make decisions that would benefit not only the seller but also the buyer. For example, if one of your children is buying the company, will that child be in a high tax bracket, perhaps 35 percent? If the seller is paying capital gains at 20 percent, then that's a total of 55 percent in taxes. Is there a way that the accountants can reduce that to 45 percent or perhaps 40 percent?

Your accountants and financial advisors will usually have several good ideas to help you structure the sale and minimize the taxes. Taxes can never be eliminated, but we definitely want to use every good technique possible for minimizing them.

FINANCIAL ADVISOR

In the past you may have worked with one or more stockbrokers or insurance agents. Some of them provide very good advice, and some don't.

When it comes to managing your net worth for the next 20 or 30 years, I normally suggest that clients seek out an independent, fee-only, registered investment advisor (RIA) with the SEC. If the person that you are working with is an RIA, then they are required to act as a fiduciary for your benefit. Your attorney and accountant are fiduciaries, and I recommend that the person that you are taking financial advice from also be a fiduciary.

Before our merger with Creative Planning, Castle Wealth Advisors specialized in working with closely held family businesses and provided independent, fee-only financial advice. You need a financial advisor who has spent years working with business owners not only discussing stocks and bonds but also making decisions about business real estate and investment real estate, such as shopping centers, apartment buildings, farmland, and other real estate investments. The financial advisor that you choose should be someone who understands the investment world and can help you analyze your personal net worth in order to help you create an allocation of assets to protect you moving forward.

Normally, business owners with a high net worth are looking for a reputable financial advisor who is backed up by a team of experts with investment and tax knowledge. These types of financial advisors always work closely with your attorneys and accountants to make sure that the dream team that you have is well coordinated and has your best interest in mind.

In 2021 we merged Castle Wealth Advisors and our affiliated companies with a larger firm known as Creative Planning, based in Kansas City, KS. With this merger, we now have access to an army of attorneys, accountants, financial experts, and investment advisors who continue to help our clients nationwide.

COMMERCIAL BANKER

If you're going to sell your company to your children or key employees, they will probably need a bank loan as part of the purchase process. The banker that you've been working with in the past may be the perfect choice to help your children get a loan from the bank for possibly 70 or 80 percent of the purchase price. Some banks like to make business loans to smaller family-held organizations and some don't. Some prefer to make loans on real estate or inventory. If your personal banker cannot help your children or key employees buy the company, then you need to look around for another bank that can help you with that process. Many banks use SBA guaranteed loans for this type of transaction.

Start talking to your bank two or three years before the sale to make sure it is interested in making a loan. If they aren't, start looking for a different type of bank for this one transaction.

CO-OP AND FRANCHISE ASSISTANCE

Some purchasing cooperatives and franchise organizations have people on their staff who can help you with the succession planning process, and they may be able to help you find a buyer. They also will need to approve any potential buyer. If you belong to either a purchasing cooperative or a franchise corporation, I suggest that you start talking to them two or three years before the sale to let them know your thoughts. They might be able to help you with a variety of matters.

TIME TO DREAM

To do it right, your team needs time—and that's why I emphasize the need to start considering your options several years in advance of the sale. Each year, the team can implement more ideas to better position your company for a profitable sale. Choose the team members early, and meet with them for two hours every six months. Tell them about the company, your family, and your goals.

Your team will not only help you sell the company and structure your documents and investments, but they will also help you structure your life and pursue your lifelong hopes. How will you go about moving to Arizona or Florida and buying a home? Should you buy it in your own name, jointly with your spouse, or in a trust?

Should you pay cash or get a mortgage? There are a lot of financial, legal, and tax considerations.

This is indeed your dream team. These are the folks who can get you started down the road toward the next phase of life for you and your family. Most business owners already have a team of advisors who have helped them to grow in business and run the company. This new team will help you with the transition as you venture forward to enjoy what you worked so hard to accumulate and accomplish.

Protection, then, is a chief aim in succession planning. When all is said and done, you want to know that your estate documents are up to date, that beneficiaries are set up properly, that your income is secure, that your spouse and heirs are protected, and that your wishes are followed and fulfilled.

This is a major operation you are going through, and you want the best advisors on your side. If you were being wheeled into surgery, you wouldn't sit up and announce, "For this, I only want the cheapest doctor." Not only do you want a surgeon, but you want one with specialized skills for your particular condition, and you want that surgeon to have the best team for this operation.

You have one life to live, and you will be selling your company only once. Do it right. The best people will cost you some money, but they will pay for themselves many times over.

CONCLUSION

I have talked to countless business owners in all 50 states, individually and at conventions, many of them nearing the time when they would like to retire and transition their company. Most of them have a basic question on their minds: "What do I do next? How do I get started on making this happen?"

I hear that question repeatedly. They're trying to figure out the end game, and they don't know where to begin. They are aware of the tax laws and the principle of capital gains, but they aren't clear how those will affect them. They know there are documents they will need, but they don't know what those are, specifically, what they would look like or who would draft them.

Between the covers of this book I have shared a multitude of ideas that I've gathered in my 50 years of experience. Even if just a few of those ideas and options change the course of your succession planning for the better, then I have served my purpose well. As you have seen from the many examples I have given, there is always more than one way to solve a problem and accomplish a goal.

Doing nothing is not an option. If you do no planning, you'll wind up paying higher taxes and getting a lower price for your company. After the transfer to the new owner, the company could end up broke within five years because the deal wasn't set up properly. If you have the right team of people helping you, your chances of success are far better.

My hope is that this book has stirred you to action. Take a step toward protecting the future—for the sake of you, your family, your business, your employees, and your community. For decades, you have worked hard to build value and serve others through your business. Now, it's time for you to pass on the business to someone else and allow it to provide for them, while the assets you earned during your time as owner provide for you.

ABOUT CASTLE WEALTH ADVISORS, LLC

In April of 2021, Castle Wealth Advisors merged with Creative Planning, one of the top independent wealth management firms in America. With that transaction, our team now has access to an army of attorneys, accountants, financial experts, and investment advisors who continue to help our clients nationwide. We continue to provide the same services we always have, moving forward under the firm name Creative Planning and Castle Valuation.

Before the merger, Castle Wealth Advisors (CWA) had grown over 48 years; specializing in providing comprehensive financial advice to individuals, families, and family held businesses in all fifty states. CWA pulled together the services of its three separate companies in order to provide strategic planning and financial management decisions tailored to each of our clients.

Castle Valuation Group prepared business valuations for established, closely held companies and provided ongoing consulting services including the construction and execution on business succession plans. Castle Financial Group was the "architect" that designed financial blueprints to protect our client's personal assets, investments, and business interests. Castle Investment Advisors was an SEC registered investment advisory firm providing investment management services. We took into account our clients' personal situations and designed well diversified portfolios that were specific to each client's needs.

Castle Wealth Advisors worked with a lot of national organizations such as large purchasing cooperatives and national franchise companies that are concerned about helping all of their members in many different ways. Many have members between 59 and 77 years of age. They know that succession or exit planning is a major concern and many of those organizations have appointed specific officers in their company to help members with financial decisions pertaining to their organization. We are lucky enough to have worked (and still do with Castle Valuation) with a lot of those national organizations to provide a wide range of financial, business valuations, and succession planning services.

Printed in the USA
CPSIA information can be obtained
at www.ICGtesting.com
JSHW012054140824
68134JS00035B/3434